Auditioning for Actor Training Programs

Elizabeth Terrel

ISBN: 978-1-63491-312-6

Published by BookLocker.com, Inc., Bradenton, Florida.

Printed on acid-free paper.

All interviews have been reviewed, edited, and approved by the interviewees. The opinions expressed are theirs. Opinions expressed by the interviewees do not necessarily reflect those of the institutions they represent as auditors, or those of the author.

BookLocker.com, Inc.
2016

First Edition

Illustrations by Elizabeth Terrel

Cover photography by Sarah West

Cover design by Todd Engel

Dedication

To Isaac, the most patient,
tolerant, and loving son I could imagine.

And to my parents, Dee and Wanda,
who moved across the country to help out
when I returned to graduate school.

The three of you have made everything possible.

Table of Contents

Introduction

Every year thousands of people audition for actor training programs. The process is important because the best programs accept a limited number of students and the audition is the major determining factor in whether one gets accepted into a program.

The audition process involves high stakes for everyone involved.

Auditioning and *Acting* are two different things. Auditioning is made better by being a good actor, but it is possible to be a VERY good actor and not audition well. Preparing a good audition is a question of knowing how to prepare and what to do in the room.

Many actors simply don't know what to do, what to show, or what is expected in the audition. Well-meaning friends and parents may try to help, but they generally don't know what's needed either - and oftentimes what they think is indicative of talent actually interferes with the authentic display of the talent that is present.

Unfortunately, many actors seem to think the auditors want to see them do "tricks" like crying on cue, doing accents, doing voices, demonstrating dramatic mood swings, or showing the wide range of characters they can play. This perception is misguided.

The auditors, most of whom are trainers in the program, are looking for a combination of qualities that will make the actor successful in their particular program. These qualities include talent, teachability, attitude, intelligence, work ethic, and future marketability. They also are looking for an actor who will be a good working member of his or her class, a pleasure to have in the classroom, and able to find professional work as an actor when he or she graduates.

Those of us auditioning people for acting training programs do not accept students based only on talent or on how badly they "want it". If we are responsible, we are also looking for people who will actually be able to *find work in the field* upon graduation. Responsible acting trainers do not want students to waste their money on an education that will not benefit them. They want their graduates to work - for the student/actor's own benefit obviously, and also for the future success of the program. One of the most common questions recruiters hear from prospective students is, "how many people are working on Broadway?" This question is innocent but misguided. There are many, many highly successful actors who don't work on Broadway. But the message is clear: actors want to know if the training program is preparing their students in a way that will allow the student to be successful. Therefore, it is important for us to select actors to train who will be successful while studying in our programs and will likely get professional work following graduation.

In talking to high school acting teachers who coach artists for undergraduate auditions, I find many of them are somewhat dismayed about what programs are looking for - often because they have seen programs accept "the wrong students" and not accept "the right ones." This book provides a reference for those teachers, for their students, and for involved parents, so everyone can be "on the same page."

Part 1 is the information you need to prepare an audition. The information is presented in a simple, informal way. I want the reader to be able to understand the process without making it more complicated than it needs to be. It is short enough to read and digest relatively quickly - for auditioning students who don't know what to do or what to expect, for well-meaning "helpers" who may not bother to read a long complicated book on "acting," and for coaches and teachers who want to provide a resource for their students that is accessible.

Part 2 contains interviews with auditors from multiple undergraduate training programs. You will likely audition for some of these people. A wide range of program sizes and types is represented.

Part 3 contains information specifically for those auditioning for graduate training programs. It contains information about expectations, requirements, and terminology needed at this level. If you are auditioning for an *undergraduate* training program, please focus on the information in Parts 1, 2, and 5. The information in Parts 3 & 4 is specific to *graduate* training auditions.

Part 4 contains interviews with auditors from multiple graduate training programs. If you are auditioning for an undergraduate training program, it is not recommended that you read these interviews right now - graduate training program requirements tend to be extremely specific and this information may be confusing.

Part 5 is written primarily for parents and supporters. At the very least, it may help you, as the actor, to have more productive conversations with those who support your efforts.

Terminology and context
This book will answer most of the questions you have about auditioning for an actor training program. I spend a lot of my time as a teacher/coach answering questions about auditioning, and have watched thousands and thousands of auditions. The purpose of this book is to help you audition to the best of your ability, and to help you through the audition process.

I will occasionally refer to the auditors (the people for whom you will audition) as *they* and sometimes as *we*. I have recruited for and taught at multiple training programs. I coach actors auditioning for training programs and professional actors auditioning in the real world. I may be on the other side of the table watching your audition one day!

Auditioning for an acting training program is very, very similar to any professional general audition in which one performs monologues. So if you're an actor doing auditions in the real world you may find the information in this book helpful. It is, however, written primarily for people auditioning for acting training programs.

By the way, I will use the term "actor" rather than the terms "actor" and "actress." It's more efficient and just as accurate. Think of an "actor" as "one who acts," rather than a masculine term.

Auditioning is a subjective process. I tell you when I'm expressing a strong personal opinion. I am not alone in my opinion, but am aware that it is my opinion that is being shared and others may disagree or not feel as strongly about it as I do.

Important clarification
The *auditionee* is you. Please note that I did not call you a contestant. This isn't a contest, though it can feel that way if you don't cultivate the right mindset. The reality is that the other auditionees are your potential friends, not your enemies. If you are accepted into the program, you will probably be in classes with some of them! So treat them with kindness.

The *auditors* are the people watching your audition. Please note that I did not call them "judges". They are not judging you. In our media culture full of shows that feature people being judged, often harshly, it's important that you understand that you are *not* being judged in that way. The auditors are looking for a lot of different things: talent, castability, flexibility as an actor, attitude, and whether what you bring to the table is a "fit" with what their training program has to offer. They are assessing you, your work, your talent, and your skill level. That is very different from the "judging" we commonly see on television.

So let's get started...

Part 1

The Audition

1-1 As you begin

This book is very practical. You will get thoroughly practical advice on how to craft a truly effective audition starting with section 1-2.

An audition is a theatrical event. Truly great theatre involves truly great acting - an indefinable quality that can really only be described as *magic*.

Acting is an art form. And for magical artistry to occur we must prepare for it and allow for it.

Most of us have seen movies where magic happened and many of us have seen it happen in the theatre.

And if you're really, really lucky you have perhaps experienced it while on stage. Most of us who pursue acting as a career have felt it. That's why we are willing to work so hard – to be able to feel it again.

The experience of magic happening on stage is something one never forgets. It's a moment, a word, and an energy that lights up the space. It is difficult to describe, but we recognize it when it happens. It's a particular sound in the way a word is spoken, or an indescribable beauty in the way light hits an actor, or an exchange between two people on stage that creates a moment of connection that everyone in the theatre can feel. It may make the audience gasp. It may raise the hairs on the back of your neck. It may seem to make time stand still. It may open up space in your soul that allows you to glimpse a truth about humanity that you have never recognized before.

Does it happen often? Not really. But when it happens it is truly magical. It is mystical. And it may change lives.

So we work incredibly hard and craft beautiful pieces of theatre and do everything in our power to create a theatrical event that can ALLOW magic to happen.

We address the STRUCTURE inherent in making theatre for this very reason: so that if we are very, very lucky we will be visited by *magic*.

This book addresses the STRUCTURE OF AN AUDITION. And if we are very lucky, magic can happen.

A useful metaphor
My favorite metaphor for this process comes from Phil Thompson, whose interview you will find in Part 4. I find this metaphor to be a perfect description of the craft of acting: What we are doing is like creating a nest. If we want to attract a particular type of bird, we need to build a particular type of nest to attract that bird.

Expanding the metaphor
Let's build a nest to attract a bird.
1) We begin by getting instructions. Perhaps we buy a book about "how to build a bird nest."
2) We follow the directions carefully, allowing for the greatest chance of success.

3) If we are very lucky a bird will come to our nest and lay eggs. We cannot control the bird's arrival, but we've crafted a beautiful place for it to visit.
4) AND someone who knows about birds and nests can look at it and recognize it as a good nest. They can see that we've built a nest that would allow a bird to come and lay eggs.

Applying the metaphor
This is what we are doing when we craft a piece of acting, which an audition is.

1) If we are very smart, we will get information on how to build a good nest. (You are reading this book, so you are already proving you are very smart.)
2) We follow the directions carefully, allowing for the greatest chance of success.
3) If we are very lucky, we will be visited by *magic*. We cannot necessarily control the arrival of magic, but we've crafted a beautiful place for it to visit.
4) AND someone who knows what it takes to craft a magical piece of acting (the auditors) can look at the audition and recognize it as a well-crafted audition. They can see that we've built a piece of theatre that will allow magic to happen.

We can't *force* magic to happen in any given moment. If we could *it wouldn't be magic*. But we can skillfully craft an audition that *allows* for magic to happen.

So this book is about how to craft a really good audition with care and attention - the way we would craft a really good nest. And as you do so…

I wish you MAGIC.

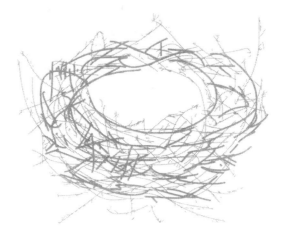

1-2 What happens in an audition

Here's the way the audition process almost always happens:

The waiting room
There is a room with people in it waiting to audition. Some will be talking to each other, some will be making faces and noises in the corner, some will be sitting quietly with their eyes closed, some will be reviewing their pieces, some will be visibly terrified, some will look like they're sitting on a bus just kind of bored. There will usually be a person sending people into the audition room. This person may be warm and friendly or cool and efficient.

The audition room
Whoever lets you into the room may introduce you. They also may not, or they may mess up your name. I recommend that you plan to introduce yourself unless *someone in charge at the audition* tells you not to.

There is usually a table with people sitting behind it - anywhere from one to eight people. The number of people isn't really important from your standpoint.

There are usually one to three people milling around doing jobs: a timer, someone letting you into and out of the room, and maybe someone bringing things to the people at the table.

It can be any kind of room, from a very small room, to a theatre, to a huge conference room. In some large rooms the auditionees do their auditions on a raised platform.

About 8 to 15 feet from the table is a place for you to stand and usually a chair that you can use if you want to.

You walk into the room.

The "timed" part:
When you get to your mark, you will:
1) Greet them with some version of "Hi, my name is ___. I am performing a piece from ___ and a piece from ___"
2) Perform your first piece
3) Transition to your second piece
4) Perform your second piece
5) Thank them
6) Exit the room

Simple. But not easy.

When does the audition start?
Technically, your audition in the room starts with your introduction or your first "acting moment". That means either when you begin your introduction or when your first piece begins. So, either the "hello" or "Hello, my name is _____" or with the breath that begins your first monologue. This means if you begin your first monologue with a moment of long, cold staring at your Imaginary Other (the person you are talking to in the monologue) before you speak, the timing begins when the stare does.

The REAL answer is that the audition begins the minute you get within walking distance of the audition site. I realize I kind of tricked you there. But you never know with whom you are interacting and what part they may play in the audition process. And trust me, if you're a diva or divo (that's my invented word), and you treat people badly, it will come back and bite you. So be a decent person. Frankly, part of me doesn't want to even tell you that, because if you're not a decent person and I'm on the other side of the table from you, I'd rather find out at your audition than after I've accepted you into my program. But I have to say it because you might be a decent person having a bad day, and if that is true I need to tell you to leave your bad day at home and bring your best self to the audition. Treat people with respect and kindness, be patient, be your best self.

How long is the audition?
This is a question you will need to find on the program's website or in their audition materials. It is vitally important. Read the instructions very carefully. If information isn't there, then call and ask, but don't call if the information is provided somewhere. Try not to annoy the people who answer the phone by calling and asking questions that are answered on the website.

Two minutes is becoming quite common. If your coach seems shocked, it's because the norm used to be three minutes. As I said earlier, we can assess your talent pretty quickly, so we really don't need three minutes. But some auditions are three minutes, so find out.

In this time, you will do all of the things in **The "timed" part** listed previously.

Timing the audition
Your audition will be timed. Generally the timing starts at your first moment of work - whether that is the first acting moment or the first word you speak when introducing yourself.

Most auditions will have either a two-minute or three minute time limit. You want to plan accordingly. What this usually means is that you need shorter pieces than you had originally thought. I encourage actors to develop 45-50 second audition pieces. It is extremely rare for you to need a piece longer than 1 minute and 20 seconds.

Timing breakdown
If the audition is two minutes long, it will break down like this:

Self introduction and piece introduction: 15 seconds
First piece: 45 seconds
Transition: 5 seconds
Second piece: 45 seconds
Thank you: 3 seconds
Total audition: 1 minute, 53 seconds

I would recommend this type of plan. If you plan an audition that takes a full two minutes, you may rush to make sure you finish your pieces on time.

It is better to get cut off than it is to rush. People get cut off all the time and it's no big deal. You won't be harshly judged for it. But you can avoid it if you choose your pieces well and make sure they're short enough.

If you do get cut off, it will almost always be with the Timer saying "Thank you". If that happens, just stop, smile, and say "thank you" to the auditors and then exit. You do not have to be embarrassed or think we are thinking negative thoughts about you because you went over time. It's not a big deal.

The components of an audition
How do you eat an elephant?
One bite at a time.
So now let's break these items that make up your experience in the room into manageable bites.

The audition space
You may be auditioning in a small room or in an auditorium. What is most common is some version of the following layout:

Finding your 'mark'

The "mark" is the place for you to stand when you begin. It is most commonly a piece of tape on the floor. You do not have to stand on the mark and do your pieces, but walk to it and then do your introduction.

It's a really great idea to put some tape on the floor and practice walking to it and stopping (called "hitting your mark") and introducing yourself. Do this in different rooms.

The mark is there for a couple of reasons that are really important.
1) The lighting is probably best there.
2) This is how far away they want you from the table.
The auditors do not want you to get super close to them. They want to WATCH you do your pieces, not feel like they are in your pieces or that your pieces are directed at them.

Stay in the general location of the mark and you will do just fine.

Using the chair

There will be a chair there that you can use or not use - your choice.
You do not need to ask if you can use the chair. It is there for you to use.
Don't abuse the chair. You can stand on it, sit on it, turn it over, or whatever. But DO NOT throw or kick the chair. It's unprofessional.

Where to look
When you walk in and when you introduce yourself, look at the auditors.

When you do each piece, direct it to your Imaginary Other (the person you are talking to in the piece). Position your Imaginary Other in a specific place.

You can put your Imaginary Other downstage center, preferably behind and above the auditors, so they can see you. The auditors are sitting, so you can let your Imaginary Other stand slightly behind them. This position lets all the auditors see your face clearly.

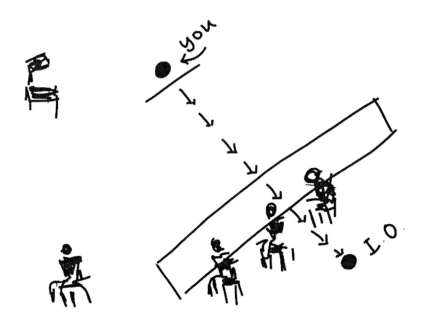

You can put your Imaginary Other in the playing space with you (in other words, between you and the auditors), at a SLIGHT diagonal. If you position your Imaginary Other far off to one side, the auditors cannot see your whole face.

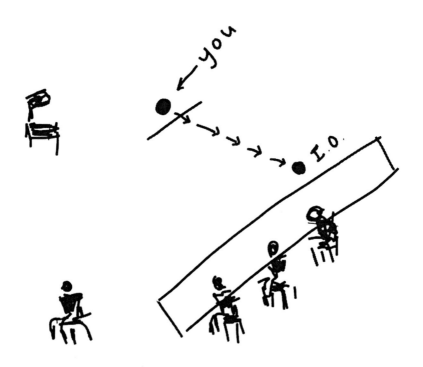

DO NOT direct the piece to the auditors, even if it's a piece where you are talking to the audience. If it's a crowd address piece, direct it to an imaginary crowd behind the auditors.

Introduction
This is your name and the pieces you will be doing. It goes something like this:

"Hi, my name is _____.
I am performing a piece from _____ by _____ and a piece from _____ by _____."

You don't have to use these exact words. You may prefer "Hello" or "Good day" or some other variation. You may prefer "I'll be doing pieces" or "I will perform" or some other variation.

Whatever you prefer, make a choice and practice that choice over and over.

Whether you should tell us what character you are doing is a personal preference.
Personally, I prefer that you not do so. If I know the play I'll recognize the character, and if I don't I won't care.
Also, if I've seen someone do a BRILLIANT Lady Anne, I am suddenly thinking about HER performance and then in my mind you are suddenly competing with her.

Please pronounce the names of the playwrights correctly. It is possible that the playwright may be in the room watching your audition. Many contemporary playwrights are on faculty at a training program.

Special note: if you are doing a piece by Shakespeare, you do not have to acknowledge the playwright. We all know his plays.

For example, if you're doing a Shakespeare monologue as one of your pieces, that introduction would sound like this:

"Hello, I'm _____. I will be performing a piece from _____ by _____ and a piece from *Romeo and Juliet.*"

Simple.

Monologues
There is a whole section on selecting and preparing your monologues. Please keep reading.

Your Imaginary Others
Imaginary Other: This is what I call the person you are talking to in your monologue.

When you are doing your piece, this person is the most important person in the room to you.

If you and I were talking in person, I would be looking at you while saying these things you are now reading. I would be watching for indications that you understood what I was saying at each moment (watching for nods, facial expressions, looks of confusion) and I would pick my words carefully to make sure *you* were understanding *me*. This conversation would be between you and me, no one else. That's the way a monologue works.

When you are speaking to your Imaginary Other with the words of your monologue, you are to do exactly the same thing. Make the Imaginary Other very, very specific and work to affect them just as you would with a real person.

Construct your Imaginary Other to be as interesting as possible. I like to use characters from movies or TV shows. I don't recommend using a real person with whom you have a real relationship, because those relationships change day to day. For example, what if you practice a monologue to your girlfriend, but then you have a huge fight right before the audition? Then what??? This is your chance to tell some movie star you are crazy about that you love him! What's not to like about that?

You can also completely make up your Imaginary Other. Take the time to make up an Imaginary Other who is just as interesting and specific as a real person. He or she must have opinions and points of view and they must have the power to walk out of the room or walk over and slap you or kiss you or hug you - just like a real person does.

The more interested you are in your Imaginary Other, the more interesting your piece will be to watch. So, as you prepare your piece, make your Imaginary Other fascinating! Imaginary Others can smile, scowl, get up to leave, jump up and down, spin in circles, cry, laugh, smirk - whatever you can imagine! They also don't have to be people - perhaps it works well for your Imaginary Other to be a huge orange beast with fangs. No one sees your Imaginary Others but you, so they don't have to be "realistic" to anyone but you.

The Transition
Between the end of your first piece and the beginning of your second, there is a transition.
1. Drop the first character

2. See your Imaginary Other for your second piece
3. Take a breath
4. Begin your piece.

Thank you
Come out of your second character and say "thank you" directly to the auditors.
Make eye contact with two or three of them. Smile. Then exit.

A note about the "thank you"
The "thank you" at the end of an audition isn't perfunctory – it's not about practicing good manners. It is an acknowledgement that you and the auditors have taken a brief, and possibly magical, journey together. You came into the room and shared yourself and your work with them. They have served as your audience, allowing this theatrical event to happen. At its best, this "thank you" is a genuine moment of gratitude for the opportunity to experience this theatrical event together.

Summary
This is how I, *as an actor*, think about the sheer mechanics of the audition:
1) I enter with my Imaginary Others and they go stand in two different places in the room. (I love that as actors we get to bring our imaginary friends to auditions with us - when I audition I never actually do it alone!)
2) I look at the auditors and have thoughts about them. (*I am truly curious about them as people.*) I take a breath, and introduce myself to the auditors.

3) I look at the 1st Imaginary Other, take a breath, and talk to him or her.
4) Then I drop that connection.
5) I look at the 2nd Imaginary Other, take a breath, and talk to him or her.
6) Then I drop that connection.
7) Then I look at the auditors and thank them. (*I sincerely thank them for giving me this opportunity to practice my craft.*)
8) Then I leave the room - and my Imaginary Others go with me.
9) Then I reward myself – more on that later.

1-3 What do you bring into the room?

"Figure out who you are and then do it on purpose." - Dolly Parton

What is unique about you?
What energy do you bring into a room?
What do you bring into a room that no one else does?
What are you 'selling'?

This is probably the hardest part for most people to figure out.

Who you are as a person and what you have to offer is something I hope you will continue to explore for the rest of your life. One of the gifts of being an actor is that we need to start asking these questions earlier than most 'normal' people and it gives us the opportunity to become more self-aware.

In my years of working with actors and non-actors as an image consultant, what I find is that most people are very aware of their weaknesses, but are not aware of their strengths. It is as if they feel that if they claimed their strengths they would somehow be bragging. Yes, we all have things about ourselves that we wish were different and things we are working to improve, but we also have gifts and positive qualities that make us unique.

As an actor, it is especially important to claim your strengths, gifts, and positive qualities.

"Who am I?" is a big question. So let's break it down a bit.

Start by asking yourself the following questions. Write down the first thing that comes to your mind.
1. What do you like about yourself?
2. What are your best qualities as a person?
3. What are your best physical features?
4. What compliments do people give you?

I would highly recommend giving your POSITIVE family and friends a questionnaire about you. (Do not give this to the aunt who doesn't like you - only to the people that you feel love you and care about you.) You will find a sample questionnaire at the end of this chapter.

When asking for direct feedback, give people a way to give you kind, positive feedback, so they will be honest
For example, you are more likely to get an honest answer to, "Is this dress flattering on me or could I make a better choice?" than you are to get an honest answer to "Do I look good in this?" or "Does this make me look fat?"
If you give someone a positive way to tell you to keep looking for a better choice, they will feel okay telling you to keep looking!

In preparation for your audition
When it comes to auditioning, the questions you want to begin with are:
"Whom do I look like?"
"How do I look like I behave?"
"When people see me, what do they expect me to be like?"

It is extremely important that you keep in mind that what you SEEM to be when you first walk into a room and what you ARE are often not the same. The way you SEEM does not define you as a human being, nor is it supposed to. But it will help steer you toward material that suits you. The auditors want to know that you know what you SEEM to be. In other words, if you appear to be a powerful, practical, direct, worldly young woman, Juliet is probably not a great choice for you. Yes, you may be an innocent, 'swept away by love' young woman on the inside, but it doesn't suit what people see when you walk in the room. Pick pieces that fit both you AND how you appear.

Making up your questionnaire
You may want to write your own questionnaire. If so, here are sample questions you might consider. You will notice a theme – you want to ask questions about how you are perceived.

1) How old do I appear to be, within 5 years? (10 years if you're close to 30 or older)
2) Which five adjectives would you use to describe me?
3) What was the first thing you noticed about me when you met me?

4) If you met me now, what would be the first thing you would notice about me?
5) If I were a car, what kind of car would I be?
6) If I were an animal, what kind of animal would I be?
7) What surprised you about me as you got to know me?
8) What sorts of activities do I look like I enjoy?
9) If you didn't know me, what would you think I do for a living?
10) What colors do I look best in?
11) What do you like best about me? What are my best qualities?
12) If I were a TV or movie character, what type of character would I be?
13) What makes me unique?

Do you see the pattern in the questions? Ask questions that will help you get information about how you are perceived in language that is useful to you, using metaphors that make sense to you.

This is also a great opportunity to find out other things, like what colors, hairstyles, styles of dress, and makeup choices your respondents think look good on you.

It may be that you will feel more comfortable using a questionnaire obviously compiled by someone else. If you'd like to distribute the following questionnaire, feel free to do so.

Audition preparation questionnaire

I am preparing to audition for acting training programs and professional productions. It would be very helpful if you would give me feedback on what SEEMS to be true about me when people first meet me. Please help me with this process by answering some questions about how I appear from the outside.

Feel free to answer these questions in as little or as much detail as you like. Any information you can give me would be helpful. Please be as honest as possible. It is important that I know how I appear to people who do not know me, as well as how I am seen by those who do.

1) How old do I appear to be? This needs to be believable and without special makeup. A range is helpful. (Example: 16-27) 17-19
18-20
19-21
21-22

2) What are five positive adjectives that describe me? If you'd like to explain one or more of them, please feel free to do so.

1. energetic, Sarcastic, creative, Sassy,
   lively
   funny.

2. Funny, outgoing, Patient, handsome, fun.

3. hard-working, funny, inteligent, caring, Social

Talented, kind, unique, charming, Pleasant.

4.

5.

3) What was the first thing you noticed about me when you met me? Well-dressed.

tall

looked like an old friend

approachable, relateable, friendly

4) If you met me now, what would be the first thing you would notice about me?

tall

Same thing, quirky, beautiful eyes

5) From looking at me, what group would you expect me to be a member of, if any? (Example: jocks, nerds, mean girls, an outsider, a loner, bad kids, druggies, etc.) Nerdy, Hipster Mashup, Jocks/nerd, Popular/band kid.

nice, cool kids, friends with everyone, likeable

6) What surprised you about me as you got to know me? Comedic abilities

more outgoing than expected.
Cool. Not a Jackass

funny, easy to talk to

Thank you so much for taking time to fill this out.

1-4 Selecting your monologues

What is a monologue?
A monologue is when a character has a large block of text that goes on for several lines.

What makes a monologue a great choice for *you*?
A great choice in a monologue is one that fits *you*.
The character is one that matches what you learned in the previous chapter – it goes with what you bring into the room.

It also has language that sounds good when you speak it and you understand the thoughts the character is expressing and the way the character is expressing them.

What makes a monologue a great monologue?
When you do a monologue, the auditors want to be able to clearly see that you are doing something specific to someone specific.

The basic questions:
1) Who are you?
2) Who are you talking to? (Who is your Imaginary Other?)
3) What do you want? (Preferably something you can get from your Imaginary Other.)
4) How do you get it?

That's it.

We want to watch you talk to a specific person, for a specific reason, about a specific thing or need.

It is best if the person you are talking to can actually solve the problem of the monologue for you.

In other words, it is better if you ask someone for a piece of bread than if you tell someone about how hungry you are, or worse yet, tell them about how hungry you were in the past.

Story monologues are just a bad idea. It's really difficult to breathe life into them because you obviously survived and are doing fine. Think about it this way: we don't watch TV shows where people talk about funny or tragic things that once happened to them - that would be boring. We watch TV shows where people are *doing actions* in situations that are funny or tragic.

Where do you find good monologues?
Plays. Read plays. Watch plays.

Can TV or movie scripts be used?
It's difficult to do it well.

The simple answer is: Some programs definitely want pieces written for the stage, so why bother with on camera scripts at all?

However, a lot of actors really want to use film scripts, so I will try to explain why this is *usually* a bad idea.

The problem is one of "stakes."

So, what *are* "stakes"?

High or low stakes refers to how much emotional and/or intellectual response a situation stimulates.

High stakes = Grandpa just died.
Low stakes = Grandpa has a cold.

Something that has "high stakes" has enough emotional or intellectual charge to elicit a physical response.

If someone told you your Grandpa just died it is unlikely that you would have no physical response whatsoever. You might cry, or freeze for a moment, or sob, or faint. The stakes of the situation justify that response.

If someone told you your Grandpa has a cold and you did any of those physical things it would look silly and fake. It would be bad acting.

The auditors are watching your whole body. So the piece you do needs to have stakes that are high enough for your whole body to be involved in some way.

Scripts written for performance on camera *can* be subtle compared to scripts written for the stage because of the nature of working with a camera. A camera can zoom in on the eyes or the face, and the audience can see that the actor cares, even if the stakes are too low to elicit a bodily response. Also, a camera can move around, and the movement of the camera adds visual interest to a story that is best told by a character just sitting and talking.

There's nothing wrong with either type of script, but a story told best with stillness and subtlety appropriate for the camera is *less likely* to be effective and moving on a stage. I'm not saying pieces that work in both situations don't exist, just that they're harder to find and prepare.

So why risk it?

What about monologue books?
There are monologue books that pull monologues from actual plays and put them in one place. Those are great, as long as you then read the actual play that the monologue was taken from once you find a monologue you like.

Monologue books that have a lot of stand-alone (not from a play) monologues are poor choices for material. Most of those monologues are stories, and a monologue where you're just telling a story is a bad choice.

Read the play
Read the entire play from which the monologue was taken.
Just do it. It's what we expect of an actor. You need to understand what is happening in the play and why your character speaks the monologue you chose. Also, if you don't read the play and we ask you about it you will feel foolish. And if you try to fake it you'll seem even more foolish. Just read the play.

Pick a character within five to ten years of your age
You will be most successful if you pick a character whose age is within five to ten years of your own age. This gives

you the best chance of being able to fully embody the emotional and intellectual life of the character.

If you are under thirty years of age, a character within five years of your age is best. If you're over thirty you can probably play someone within ten years of your own age effectively.

Pick a monologue you like

Pick a piece you *enjoy*. You will work with it a lot and you will perform it many times. In the ideal world, once you find a really great monologue, you can do it for ten to fifteen years, so pick one you *love*.

Pick monologues that deal with things you understand

Select monologues that allow you to realistically imagine your way into the experience of the character. You have been scared in your life, so you can imagine that. You have felt powerless and joyful and excited. You have celebrated, and bragged, and asked for help, and run away. You can imagine yourself into the reality of those situations.

Extremely high stakes situations can be tricky. If you choose to do monologues that are potentially tricky, *really* take the time to imagine yourself in the circumstances of the monologue and of the situation.

1) *Death can be tricky.* Maybe you have an experience that will help you with it, in which case, go for it.
2) *Parenthood can be tricky for young actors.* If you're a parent or caregiver of a child, yes, by all

means pick a monologue in which you are speaking to a child or dealing with someone concerning your child. If you're not a parent or a caregiver, know that you will need to invest time imagining your child in great detail and how you might feel as a parent.

Monologues do not need to be super intense
This is a hard one for most aspiring actors to accept. The auditors can see what they're looking for even though you're not experiencing the worst moment of your life. You do not have to show them you can cry or scream or act crazy.

Auditors watch a lot of super intense monologues, and frankly, the ones in which the auditionee talks to another person about something they care about without screaming or crying is often a HUGE relief.

Do not scare the auditors
Pick pieces that show range without "charging the table" (getting too close to the auditors), making the auditors wonder if *you* really are crazy, or making them uncomfortable to be in the room with you. Enter and leave as a normal person.

Avoid pervert monologues
Don't play a pedophile. Don't talk about raping or killing people. Don't play a bigot or a truly reprehensible human being. If you select a monologue that makes the auditors uncomfortable they will wonder why you chose it. They will also wonder if there is something wrong with you.

Avoid monologues with the n-word
This is so offensive to so many people, that it's just a bad choice. If you just *have* to do a particular monologue, edit if at all possible.

Avoid monologues with excessive explicit swearing
I am not saying not to do monologues with swearing in them – we are not prudes.

But avoid monologues that are all about the swearing – they tend not to be very interesting. We don't need to see how "edgy" you can be.

Keep your clothes on
Do not strip down to do a piece. You can take off a jacket or a scarf or your shoes. That's it.

The chair
You don't have to use the chair. But it's fun to use the chair if you do it right.

How many ways can you use a chair? How many ways can you sit on it? Lean on it? Stand on it? Can you move it and talk at the same time? Experiment! Try new things!

The chair is a useful tool that lets us see how you move, how you think, and how your creativity and movement work together. I'd use it if I were you.

Do not throw the chair or abuse the space!
Don't throw, kick, hit, push, or damage the chair in any way. It is unprofessional. Just don't do it. At all. Ever.

Common questions about monologues
What about "overdone" monologues?

There are monologues that auditors see a lot. If you can find something we are less likely to see over and over, that's great. But it is hard to find classical monologues we haven't seen before. The monologues that most often fall into the category of overdone monologues are Launce from *Two Gentlemen of Verona* and Phoebe from *As You Like it.*

The general rule of thumb is that if you do a monologue really well, the auditors are going to see what you can do, even if they've seen that piece many times.

What if my friend and I do the same monologue?

It's not ideal, but it happens.
Keep in mind that the auditors don't know which auditionees are your friends.
Do the monologues that are good for you and don't waste energy competing with anyone.

What does "contrasting monologues" mean?

Most programs request that you perform two contrasting monologues. A lot of actors are confused about what "contrasting" means.

There are some obvious answers to the question of contrast:
-Classical (Shakespeare or similar) versus Contemporary (which usually means a play less than 50 years old)
-Comedy versus Tragedy

It's not quite that simple, though. You also want two pieces that show you trying to get what you want in *two different ways*.

One piece is usually from a comedy and the other is usually from a drama.

Do I have to do a Shakespeare (or classical) piece?
This is one of those questions that is probably best answered on the program's website, in the audition materials, or with a phone call. Some undergraduate training programs want to see if you can handle classical language and some don't.

If I do a Shakespeare piece am I supposed to sound British?
No. Sound like yourself.

What if I'm not funny? How do I do a comedic monologue?
A comedic monologue is not about you making jokes and being funny. It's about a character in a funny or light-hearted situation. You may be a "straight man" type, which means we will enjoy watching you deal in a serious way with a humorous or absurd situation.

Where to find plays and audition pieces
Ask for recommendations from people you know
This is an easy place to start. Explore the ideas you get, but don't stop there. Do the other three things below as well.

Go to libraries and bookstores
Go to the library or to the bookstore.
Go to the "plays" section.
Open a lot of plays and read the character descriptions.
See if there are any characters that sound right for you.
If there are, flip through the play and find a monologue that character speaks.
Do you like it?
If so, check out the book. Or order it. Or if you really, really like the monologue, buy the play.

"Read around" a playwright
When you find a play you like, check out everything the playwright has ever written. Most playwrights have common themes, language, and types of characters. And they have some plays that are better than others. Which means that a play that gets staged a lot probably has multiple "brothers and sisters" - plays by the same playwright that for some reason aren't performed as much. Those plays likely have some monologues you would like.

IBDB and IMDB backwards
You have probably been told something like "you make me think of…" that led to the name of someone famous.

You can use these comments as a way to build a web of actors with whom you may share characteristics that will help you find material.

Here's an example:
1) "You make me think of Woody Harrelson."
2) IMDB (International Movie Database) and IBDB (International Broadway Database) Woody Harrelson and get every role he's ever done
3) Search those plays, movies, and roles and make a list of the other actors who have done those roles. As you can imagine, this is easier with plays than movies, but there are movies based on plays that may lead you to cast lists for other productions.
4) Search other roles those actors have played.
5) You now have a huge list of actors (many of whom were previously unknown to you) who may also have something in common with you, and lists of roles that may be good for you.
6) Check out those roles and plays and see if something appeals to you.

This process takes time but often yields a large quantity of material for you to check out. If you continually follow up on those "you make me think of" comments you can find some unexpected material.

Jim
- Role 1
- Role 2
- Role 3
  - Joe
  - Will
  - Tito
    - Role 4
    - Role 5
    - Role 6

this may also
be a great
role for Jim!

What if I find a monologue I like from a play that isn't really very good?
This happens all the time. Do the monologue. Some not-so-great plays have some great characters and monologues in them.

What makes a monologue really great?
The short answer is you - if you show through the piece, it can be great.

What makes it a truly great audition piece is how you prepare it. If the auditors can see you *doing different things to get what you want*, that is excellent. In an ideal situation, a 30 second monologue will show 3 different ways of getting what you want (called a tactic or an action). Let them see you change tactics. The first change should ideally happen within the first 10 seconds.

For example, if you're doing a piece in which you are trying to get someone to not shoot you, *how many ways* can you get them to not shoot you?

If someone were about to shoot *me*, I would pull out all the stops! I would no doubt plead, beg, scare them, seduce them, lecture them, charm them, educate them, make them feel important... you name it! I would try any and every thing to get them not to shoot me. Now wouldn't that make a great monologue? If I *really work* to get my imaginary other not to shoot me for 30 seconds, the auditors have seen at least 3 or 4 ways that I would behave in that situation. They know a lot more about me when I am done. That is the goal. And that would be a killer audition piece.

Summing it up
You are going to work very hard to find great pieces that show *you* and then work really hard to make them *yours*. Ideally, you are looking for monologues that, once you have worked them a great deal, will *feel like you talking to someone*. You are going to work hard to make this seem natural.

Once you've really done your work, it feels like YOU saying these words. The auditors can see YOU through the monologue in how you inhabit the character, and also by the type of monologue you selected.

1-5 Preparing your monologues

Memorizing
This has to be done. It must be word perfect. It is work for most people. Just do it.

Coaching
If you can, hire a coach. Even an hour working with someone who can help you with your monologues and give you expert feedback is useful. You will probably need to pay a coach - how much is dependent on the market you're in - but it is money invested in your future.

You may want to reach out to faculty at the institution you're auditioning for and see if there is someone who can watch your pieces and give you feedback. This can be a good way to get some help and also get to know someone on the faculty. Don't be offended if they cannot help, but it never hurts to ask as long as you do it in a respectful manner that acknowledges their time constraints and gives them a gracious way out in case they don't have time.

Practicing in front of people
Perform your audition for anyone who will watch. You want the experience of doing your monologues in front of people. It's a good idea to let your audience know that you aren't really looking for them to "help" you, so they don't need to feel pressured to give you feedback.

Is it a good idea to practice in front of a mirror?
No. When you do your pieces, the only thing you should be focused on is the person you are talking to (the

Imaginary Other) and what you want. If you practice in front of a mirror it is hard to avoid thinking about how you look when doing your pieces.

Should you use an accent or dialect?
No. The auditors want to see you, not your facility with a dialect. So pick pieces that sound good in your natural accent. (And, yes, we do all have an accent.)

Use your own voice
It is common for young actors to develop a "stage voice" that doesn't sound like their real voice. It's usually slightly higher in pitch for women and usually lower in pitch for men than their natural speaking voice. It often has a slightly more "careful" sound than the actor's natural speech. Sometimes young actors think that is what auditors are looking for. It is not. If you are in the habit of doing a "stage voice," work to overcome it.

If you are considering doing monologues you learned with a "stage voice," you may want to pick new monologues and focus on learning them in *your voice*. It might be easier than overcoming vocal habits you developed when you originally performed the monologue.

1-6 What to wear

What you wear matters.

The right clothing choice sends the message that you care for yourself, value yourself, and think positively about yourself and your body.

The wrong clothing choice can literally make it impossible for auditors to see who you are and how they will be able to utilize you in their program.

Wear clothing that looks good on you and shows your best self. It is not necessary to dress like you're going to a wedding or a dinner party.

The general rule of thumb is that the auditors should be able to see the most attractive version of *you* without a lot of distraction. They should be able to see the *shape* of your body, but *don't show lots of skin*. You are the size and shape you are. Be proud of it.

Auditioning is a little like dating: you do not want to fool someone into picking you. Sooner or later they will figure out who you are! Be yourself. Allow them to see who you are – the shape, size, and personality of you.

If you wear baggy clothing, they cannot tell your actual size. This is not good.

If you have piercings, with the exception of earrings for women, it really is best to take them out.

All the auditors know about you is what you show them. Avoid being "ironic" because they don't know you well enough to know what you're doing, and they will probably think you're serious.

Here are some general guidelines, beginning with special considerations for women and for men.

Guidelines for women
Undergarments
Wear a bra – a good bra that does not show (underwear should stay "under")
No panty lines
If you wear stockings, have an extra pair in your audition bag

Skirts or pants?
If you have great legs and wear skirts all the time, wearing a skirt is fine UNLESS you are going to sit on the floor, sit with your legs apart, or do some physical thing that will make the auditors wonder if you will accidentally flash them. You want them watching your work, not worrying about whether they will see more of you than they bargained for.

Pants or slacks are also fine. Wear what you are most comfortable wearing.

What to wear on top
There is a lot of flexibility here, but these are some general guidelines:
♦ Solid colors are best – it is hard to compete with a print.

♦ If you wear a blouse with a button front, make sure it does not bag, sag, or pull.

♦ Sweaters are fine, but avoid bulky sweaters that hide the shape of your body.

♦ Baby doll dresses and garments with an empire waist (starts at the bra line and then falls loosely) will look like maternity clothes to most people over 35, which is the age of most of those for whom you will audition.

♦ If you like T-shirts that's okay, but they need to be in good shape, a good color, and it's nice if they are heavy enough that we can't see through them under the lights.

♦ Jackets, cardigans, vests, over-blouses, shawls, and scarves are not a good idea. They *hide* you. If you *must* wear a jacket, it should fit your body nicely - not be baggy or saggy or make you look bigger than you are. Like everything else you choose to wear, a jacket or sweater should not *hide* your body.

♦ Whatever you choose should be flattering, allow the shape of your body to be seen, not show your bra or a great deal of cleavage, and cover your midriff.

Draw attention to your best features
Use your clothing choices to draw attention to the parts of your body and your shape that you feel best about.

For example, if you have a smallish waist (an "hourglass" or "pear-shaped" figure) a belt may flatter the shape of your body by defining your waist. If you do not have a smallish waist it is probably best to skip the belt. It does not "create" a defined waist to add a belt - in fact, it can detract from your better features.

If you have great legs, draw attention to them! Wear a narrower cut pant to show off long, thin legs. Or wear a skirt that shows off your shapely legs without being too short.

Or maybe you have a beautiful neck, in which case pick a neckline that draws attention to it.

Get the idea?

"Drawing attention to" versus "exposing"
Keep in mind that "drawing attention to" and "exposing" are not the same thing.

You can allow the shape of your body to show by choosing clothing that *skims the contours of your body*, rather than exposing your skin.

It is distracting to show too much skin. If you choose clothing that shows a great deal of cleavage, or your midriff, or is very short, or has a deeply slit skirt, it makes everyone uncomfortable.

Shoes
Your audition is about you, not about your shoes.
I have seen some awesome shoes at auditions, but I do not remember whose feet they were on. You want the auditors to remember *you*, not your shoes. And your shoes absolutely, positively should not be clunky.
♦ High heels: *Very* few people can walk well in a heel that is over 3" high. It is extremely important that you can move well in the shoes you choose.

♦ Boots: A sleek boot that is fitted at the ankle and calf can be a good choice. Boots that are chunky or bulky are not a good choice – they will obscure the shape of your leg and ankle.

♦ Character shoes and dance shoes: If a pair of character shoes is all you have, they are acceptable, but not preferred. Even musical theatre people would rather see you in street shoes for song and monologue auditions. Jazz booties, jazz sneakers, and actual ballet slippers are for dancing, not for auditions. Wear shoes.

♦ Sneakers: Gym shoes are not for auditions.

♦ Flip-flops: NO. Just no. They are noisy and distracting.

Makeup

Makeup is best if you look like YOU on a great day. In other words, you will probably want to wear a bit of makeup (at least mascara and some lip color or gloss) for polish. Avoid extremes - makeup should accentuate your facial features, not hide them or distract from them.

Guidelines for men
Slacks? Jeans? Trousers?

Auditioning for an acting training program is a fairly traditional auditioning environment. If you choose to audition in jeans, it is best if they are clean and in very good shape. Slacks or trousers are good choices.

Shorts and sweat pants are to be avoided.

Suits You do not need to wear a suit. In fact, they are too dressy for an audition and affect your ability to move freely. The jacket also hides the shape of your body.

What to wear on top

There is a lot of flexibility here, but these are some general guidelines:

♦ Solid colors are the safest choice – it is hard to compete with a bright print.

♦ A button up shirt is fine – it should not sag, bag, or pull.

♦ Sweaters are fine, but avoid bulky sweaters that hide the shape of your body.

♦ If you like T-shirts that's okay, but it needs to be in good shape, a flattering color, free of words and pictures, and heavy enough that we can't see through the shirt under the lights.

♦ Ties are statement pieces. Make sure, before you wear one, that you are making a statement you want to make.

Shoes

♦ Wear shoes you like that you can walk well in, and that look good.

♦ Shoes should be similar in "dressiness" to the pants you wear. If you wear dressy pants or suit pants you need hard-soled shoes. Absolutely no sneakers with slacks or dress pants! There are a select few companies that make extremely high-quality, expensive "sneakers" – if you wear these you know what they are and you know what to wear them with.

♦ No sandals, no flip-flops.

♦ No gym shoes!

Socks

Socks that are not dark are a fashion statement. Make sure it's one you want to make. Colored socks say something along the lines of "hipster or fashion guy" and white socks say something along the lines of "aspiring geek and proud of it". That is fine if that's who you are, but give it thought and be sure that's a message you want to send.

Guidelines for both women and men
Hair
Your face should be the focal point, not your hair. Your hair should be out of your face and should *stay* out of your face. Use hairspray, use barrettes, use hair glue - whatever it takes to get your hair out of your face and keep it there.

Also, don't get your hair colored a wild color to impress the auditors with your creativity, or try some new color for the audition. Generally speaking, people are most castable with a "normal", flattering hair color. Odds are you were born with the best hair color for you.

To summarize:
1) Your clothing should flatter you but not hide your shape.
2) Showing lots of skin is inappropriate and makes everyone uncomfortable.
3) If you are going to get on the floor or put a leg up on a chair, don't wear a skirt.
4) Shorts are too casual, as are tank tops and extremely casual t-shirts.
5) If you wear jeans they must be in very good condition.
6) Jackets, cardigans, over-shirts, scarves, and so forth are a bad idea because they hide the shape of your body.

7) Shoes should match the dressiness level of your clothing: if you wear dressy pants, a suit, or a skirt, sneakers are not appropriate.
8) Contrasting socks or tights are a fashion statement and send a definite message.
9) You don't have to be "dressed up," but this IS a special occasion and it is not the time to look like you just rolled out of bed.
10) Your face needs to be easily visible – get and keep your hair out of your face.
11) I think it should be obvious, but in case it is not, don't wear a hat of any kind.

1-7 Warming up your body and your voice

A proper and complete warm up will prepare your body and voice. It will facilitate expressive movement and expressive, articulate voice work. When you are properly warmed up you will feel open and flexible, and your body and voice will feel *free*, not *tired*. A good warm up leaves you feeling "all revved up and ready to go."

Warming up is like bathing – we need to do it regularly. It is not something we can do a few times, master, and then stop doing. Actors must warm up regularly just as we must shower or bathe regularly.

Warm up before you practice as well as before you perform. If you warm up before you practice, your practice time will be much more productive – a warmed up body and voice are more expressive and you will work in a healthier way.

At the *very least*, on the day of the audition you need to warm up physically and vocally. Do a full warm-up early in the day, and then do whatever you can (whatever space allows) shortly before your audition.

Ideally, you already know warm-up exercises that prepare your body and voice to do acting work. If you do, practice your warm up daily, before you practice, and before you perform.

If you don't have a warm up you already know and practice, this is a good time to learn one. If you can take a class between now and your audition, do so. If you don't have time or access to a class, see the **very basic warm up*** at the end of this section.

Why is this so important? Because you can't do your best acting work if your body and voice are restricted. You may have done all your other preparation well and you may be a gifted actor, but if your body and/or voice are not warmed up enough to allow a full range of expression, the auditors can't tell how good you are.

You may also notice, as you look at the auditor interviews in Part 2 and Part 4, that many of us who recruit actors for training programs are voice and/or movement specialists. Those of us who specialize in voice and movement are particularly sensitive to whether you have prepared your body and voice for work. So it's a good idea to make sure you have done so.

On the day of your audition
1) Wake up early enough so that you will feel great by the time of your audition.
2) Do what you know for your body - ideally, a warm up for acting work or the **very basic warm up***.
   If you are not practicing an actors' warm up, do what you know for your body. If you're a runner, run. If you're a dancer, martial artist, swimmer, etc. prepare your body with warm-ups you do for whatever activity you do. If you're a yogi, do some yoga. Do what you can to stretch, open, and expand your body.
   Note: if you're not in the habit of moving much, you might want to start moving a bit more in some way between now and the audition. What you *do*

not want to do on the day of your audition is a movement sequence you've never done before that makes you tense, weak, sore, stressed, or tired.
3) If you're a singer, warm up your voice to sing.
4) Talk to someone you like – get your speaking voice warm. If no one is around, call someone. Talk to someone you enjoy and have a fun, expressive conversation – this is not the time to risk a disagreement that will leave you vocally stressed.

*Very basic warm up

If you have weeks or months until your audition, you have time to learn a warm up. For you, I have prepared this very basic warm-up sequence. Do it every day before you practice, and do it before you audition.

RELEASE
1. Lie on the floor in Gingerbread Man position: on your back, with your legs separated and your palms facing up.
2. Squeeze your eyes and mouth closed tightly. Then open your eyes wide and open your mouth wide and stick out your tongue. Then close your eyes and let your mouth/jaw relax, but continue to keep your mouth open – let your jaw hang down toward the floor – not forcing it open, just letting it hang open - I call this "duh" face.
3. Wiggle your arms and legs and torso all over the place and let your body make silly, goofy, sounds.
4. Return to Gingerbread Man position with your eyes closed and your jaw released in "duh" face.

5. Lie there for 5 minutes, ideally, and just let your body melt into the floor.

OPEN
   1. If you remember stretching exercises from gym classes or dance classes, do them now.
   2. Stand up and wiggle your body and shake every part of your body you can shake. While you are doing this, make "aaaahhh" sounds with your voice and let the shaking of your body make your voice shaky, too.

SIRENS
   1. Start making sound on what feels like a "low" pitch to you. Then let your voice go up "high" and come back down. This perhaps sounds like a police or fire siren.
   2. Do this on a singing sound - even if you're not a singer.
   3. Do this on a speaking sound - even if you are a singer.

   Note: Sirens are not just for singers! You may make some truly awful sounds while you are doing sirens. Good! The point is to warm up your voice, not to sound "pretty."

Please remember that the goal is to warm up, not strain, your body and your voice. If anything feels distinctly uncomfortable, leaves your voice feeling tired or strained, or makes you feel pain in your body, you are overdoing it.

If you do these very simple exercises every day, you will find your body becomes looser and more flexible, and you will find your voice starts to feel looser and more flexible as well.

I realize that these things are distinctly uncool. Keep reading! Actors are only cool on the red carpet...

1-8 Entering the room

Before you enter the room:
1) Stop for a moment.
2) Take a breath and let it out.
3) Have a positive thought about yourself.
4) Allow yourself to feel excited and curious about whatever will happen in that room.

This sounds easy, but it takes practice. So practice.

Then… take a breath as you walk through the door…

As you enter
As you walk through the door, take a breath in through your mouth. This will help relax your body and your mind and will help you "land" in the room.

Look at the people in the room. Make eye contact with two or three of them.

Be CURIOUS about the people in the room:
> What are they wearing?
> What order did they sit in?
> Do you like their shoes?
> Do they seem to like each other?
> Are they looking at you or are they working on something?
> Do they work on computers or do they write on paper?

It doesn't matter what you are curious about – whatever it is that you notice about people, notice about *these* people.

What this accomplishes
First of all, every second you spend thinking about them is one less second you have to worry about what they are thinking about you.

Being self-conscious is just that: being SELF CONSCIOUS.
If we are conscious of other people, we do not have time to be conscious of ourselves.

The other really valuable thing this does is help you see the auditors as PEOPLE, which is just what they are. They are people. They are people who like actors and like training actors. They want you to do well. They are looking at you for your potential and your talents. They are truly looking for your very best qualities!

Some of these people may become very important to you in your life. They may be your teachers. They may open doors for you. They may help you become the artist and actor you are meant to become.

MEET them.
TALK to them.
INTRODUCE YOURSELF to them.

They have been waiting to meet you. Be sure you take a moment before you begin your monologues, and really MEET THEM.

*To read more on this subject, watch for **How To Enter The Room** - coming soon.*

1-9 Working pieces

Important to know
If the auditors want to "work a piece" with you it probably means they already like you, so just go for it!
(But if they don't ask to "work a piece" it isn't bad.)

What "working a piece" means
This is when auditors ask you to do one of your monologues (pieces) and then they *coach* you, asking you to try different things with the monologue.

What "working a piece" is not
They are not fixing your monologue. They are not fixing you. Do not assume there is anything wrong with what you were doing.

Maybe you will discover something new about your piece, but maybe you won't. They aren't necessarily trying to make anything better at all. In fact it may make it worse – that's okay.

Don't worry at all about it. Just do it.

What "working a piece" shows them about you
Probably they are trying to see any one of a number of things about you.
Possibilities are:
1) Can you change what you have practiced? Sometimes actors practice a lot and perhaps get really good at a monologue, but when asked to do something different, they can't change at all. They may want to see if you can change.

2) Are you "game"? They may want to see if you are just *willing to play*. Are you willing to let go of your preconceived ideas of what your monologue is and try something new? They may ask for something totally ridiculous just to see how you think and how far you are willing to go with a piece.
3) Can you make different choices? Maybe the things you showed in your two monologues were very similar. They may want to see if you can do a different type of acting. You have monologues memorized, so it is logical to work with the pieces you already know and see if they can get you to do something different.
4) Can you "work off of" a real person? They want to see how you connect with a real person when you act. They may have you work with a student actor in the room or with an auditor. They may ask you to do the monologue TO A PERSON.
5) They may be looking at your skill set and possibilities. They may want to see a range of movement or voice possibilities.

When it comes to working pieces there are some very important things to understand:

Let go of the need to be "cool"
It will help you in the preparation process if you accept one very important thing:

Actors are only cool on the red carpet.

We are used to seeing actors on TV and in magazines all dressed up, looking beautiful and suave. We are used to seeing them in fully realized performances on screen and on stage. But to turn in amazing performances they worked incredibly hard. They struggled and tried many things that didn't work. They played a LOT and did some things that were ridiculous. The very cool finished product only happened because they were willing to look and feel very *un*cool at some point in the process.

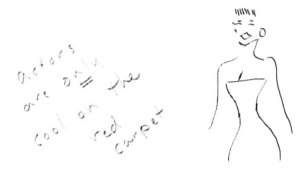

Be willing to work hard and to feel uncool and to try crazy new things.

It's a paradox: If you are willing to be uncool, *that makes you cool.*

Coaching is not criticism
They may be trying new things just for the heck of it. They may be checking out what else you can do, or how far you will go toward simplicity (quiet, matter of fact, non-dramatic), or if you will go completely over-the-top.

PLAY
If they ask for something different, give them something very different. They may want to see how your mind works, or how brave you are, or how willing you are to just plain PLAY.

They may also be checking your attitude – are you willing to let go of "cool" and try something new that may be awful?

Can you laugh at yourself?

An auditor once asked me to do a classical piece as if I was underwater. I think it's possible that he saw S.C.U.B.A. on my special skills and it gave him the idea, and he thought it would be fun. He probably wanted to see how far I would go. It was a chance to play, so I *went for it*. I was totally uncool and it was undoubtedly *the worst Tamora monologue ever*. He and I had a blast. It was awful but it was also really fun and the auditor and I laughed and had a great time. He ended up doing it *with* me.

He also made me an offer!

What you will learn
You will find out a lot about the auditors if you get the chance to work pieces with them. You will find out something about how they work. You will learn something about whether this is someone you enjoy and whether you want to work more with them.

The guy who did pretend Shakespearean S.C.U.B.A. with me? Ultimately I accepted an offer from another program, but he and I are now friends.

1-10 Interviews

You may be interviewed as part of the audition process. Many undergraduate training programs and most graduate training programs incorporate an interview as part of the audition process. Some acting training courses conduct interviews with prospective students in lieu of asking them to perform a traditional audition.

An interview may take place in person, on the phone, or via Skype or FaceTime.

An interview is a conversation. It is not a test. Your "job" in an interview is to be yourself, be present, listen, share, and communicate.

There is absolutely no point in pretending to be someone you're not in an interview, or in trying to hide behind answers that seem like the "right" answers. If you are accepted into the program, all will be known sooner or later anyway!

Basically, preparation for an interview involves thinking about two distinct things: 1) the program and the trainers and 2) yourself and how you view yourself and your goals.

Think about the program and the trainers
Odds are that in the interview you will be asked if you have any questions. You should have questions.

What do you want to know about the program?
What do you want to know about the trainers?

Prepare questions – REAL questions, not just made-up stuff you don't really care about. What sorts of things do you care about? What do you want to know about the people who may be training you?

Research the program. Know what their focus is. It is a waste of your time and theirs to ask things that you would know if you had taken time to read the website. So read the website, research the trainers, and learn as much as you can about the program for which you are auditioning. Then when you ask questions you will ask *good* questions.

Think about trainers and teachers you have had that have impacted you positively. What made them good teachers for you? What qualities did they possess that helped you learn?

The interview is an excellent chance to ask questions of your prospective trainers. Use this opportunity to ask what you really want to know.

Think about yourself
Odds are that you will be asked some questions about yourself.

Preparing for auditions and interviews provides an excellent opportunity to explore your own desires, wants, hopes, needs, and creative processes. The following questions are worth consideration. Take your time. Give these things deep thought. Really take advantage of this opportunity to know your artistic and creative self better.

Why do you want to be an actor?
What is your ultimate dream?
Who are your heroes?
What feeds you creatively?
What do you like to do *other than* acting?
What stories do you want to tell?
What lights a fire in your soul?
What is your favorite play?
What is your favorite movie?
What are your strengths?
What are areas in which you want to grow?
What is the most amazing moment you have had in the theatre?
What has shaped your ideas of what it is to be an artist?
What is it about acting that enriches your life?
Why are you seeking further training?
What do you hope to learn?

Asking yourself these questions will lead to you to think more deeply about your artistic journey, goals, and vision.

Please know that there aren't "right" or "wrong" answers to any of these questions. You can't really "fail" an interview. The more honest and open the exchange, the more successful your interview will be.

One caution
The interview is *not* the time to express your frustrations with past training programs or teachers. Your mom was right: If you don't have something nice to say, it's best to say nothing at all.
Focus on the positive.

Notice what the auditors in Part 2 and Part 4 share about interviews

Some of the auditors share quite a lot about the interview portion of the audition process. Their insights can certainly provide some useful things to think about as you prepare for this part of the process.

1-11 Frequently Asked Questions

What if they do a group warm-up or exercises?
Do it just like you would if you were in a class. Be yourself. Do the exercise.

Focus your attention on the exercise and the people teaching it and doing it.

There may be people watching, but they are irrelevant to you while you are doing the exercise.

Don't try to stand out or try to guess what they are looking for.

They want to see who you are. You just be yourself!

How do I deal with stage fright?
There are many ways to deal with stage fright. I will list some of the ones I find most effective here.

1. *Notice that stage fright and excitement feel exactly the same.* This realization is the single most effective way to deal with stage fright.

StageFright = Excitement

Once we realize that it feels just like excitement, then it's just a matter of choosing to call it excitement.

2. *Relax and release tension.* Sit in a chair or lie on the floor and close your eyes and breathe. Just breathe. Picture yourself on a beach or under a tree or lying in your bed, relaxed and happy and warm. All performers ought to invest time in discovering their most effective "happy place" images - the places in our minds where we can go when the stakes get high and we need a place to relax. Your actor imagination can be either your best friend who soothes you or your worst enemy who frightens you. Let it be your best friend.

3. *Be curious about the people around you.* Stop thinking about yourself and how you're doing. Notice the people around you, notice the people you're auditioning for, notice the space you're in. Don't ask them questions or bug them, but *wonder*, be *curious*. The extra side benefit of this is that interest in others makes you a more interesting person!

4. *Decide to have fun.* Yes - decide. An actor's life is audition after audition after audition. The sooner you decide to enjoy the process, the sooner you will start to enjoy your life. You've chosen this as a way of life - you might as well find the fun in it!

5. *"Screw it! I did my work! Bring it on!!"* This is a slightly altered version of deciding to have fun. Once you've prepared and are waiting to go into the audition room, there's nothing left to do but to DO IT.

1-12 Preparing your "stuff" for the audition Headshot, Resume, Statement of Purpose, Audition Bag

Your Headshot

You will need a picture of yourself, called a "headshot" because it is a picture of your head, neck, and perhaps upper torso only. How professional it needs to be depends on the type of school you are applying to. For most undergraduate programs, you will need a good picture that looks like you. For graduate programs, you will want a professional headshot.

You Look Just Like Your Head Shot

The number one, most important thing about a headshot is that is looks just like you. The best compliment an actor can receive is, "You look just like your headshot."

Your hair should be the same color and basically the same style as it will be when you audition. So, no major hair color changes and no drastic style changes. This means don't go from long hair to a very short cut without a new headshot.

You do not have to be smiling, but you do want to appear approachable and friendly.

Silly, but it has to be said: You should not look like you are naked. In other words, a camisole is better than a strapless top in which straps don't show. Those little straps make a big difference!

If you're having headshots taken, here are some basic guidelines:
1) Meet with the photographer ahead of time and make sure you are comfortable with him/her.
2) Wear a color that is flattering.
3) Wear your makeup the way you will at the audition.
4) Ladies, a little lip color finishes your look. That said, don't wear bright lipstick in your headshot if you won't wear it to your auditions.
5) Solid colored clothing is generally better than prints.
6) Accessories should not be distracting. Avoid wild earrings and distracting ties.
7) White is not your best shirt choice - it can be harder to light. But if your photographer can manage it, it is okay to wear it if you really want to. Ask.
8) Hands in headshots can be distracting.
9) Photos in which you are hunched over tend to be unflattering.

Your Resume

Your resume is a list of your personal assets, contact information, and previous acting experience. It tells the auditors what work you've done and what training you've had.

The font should be 10-14 point and easy to read.

Your resume should fit on a single page. This means you may not be able to fit every role you've ever played on it – so list your favorites.

Arrange your resume in a format that is easy to read. You want the auditors to be able to *quickly* skim your resume and get the information they need so they can watch your audition! Columns need to be straight, headings need to be clear, and it needs to be thoroughly proofread – no typos!

Your resume should have the following information:
1) Name at the top
2) Height
3) Hair color
4) Eye color
5) Voice type if you're a singer: Soprano, Mezzo Soprano, Contralto, Tenor, Baritone, Bass, etc.
6) Email address – Your email address needs to be professional – a professional name and not school-related. It should also forward to your phone if possible so you can be reached easily and respond in a timely manner.
7) Phone number – This is your cell phone number so you can respond in a timely manner.
8) Theatrical experience in list form: Play, Role, Venue, Director
9) On camera experience, if applicable: Project, Project Type, Role, Producer, Director
10) Education: workshops, teachers, anything that tells how you have been trained
11) Special Skills: this is a list of things you can do. Be sure to list things that are cool and unusual. Make

sure you can really do them, right then if they ask you. For example, the list may go something like this:

Special Skills: Horseback riding (Western), Motorcycle license, SCUBA, yoga (expert), Russian (fluent), burp loudly on cue, salsa dancing (intermediate)

If you are applying to a program right out of high school you are going to have a lot of high school productions on your resume and that is fine.

As you list productions, put the ones of which you are proudest at the top. You do not need to list them in chronological order.

Here is a sample:

Alice Somebody

Height: 5'9"	Hair: Brown	Eyes: Green	Voice: Mezzo –Soprano
Email: asomebody@gmail.com			Phone: 555-222-1212

Stage

Thoroughly Modern Millie	Millie	Main Street Theatre	Joe Anybody
Mame	Vera	2nd Street Theatre	Nel Anybody
Oklahoma	Ado Annie	2nd Street Theatre	Max Anyone
To Kill A Mockingbird	Boo Radley	Big Plans Theatre	Cheri Person

On Camera

Aspirin Commercial-Regional Spot	Consumer	1st Street Company	Jim Film
Chairs & Tables-SAG Feature Film	Sammie	Main Street Film	Jo Director
Cleaning the Floor-Student Film	Floor Lady	Film School	Bev Student

Training

Voice for the Stage	Local Theatre Studio	Stuart People
Acting On A Big Stage	Acting Studio	Clay Goodguy
Ballet	V's Dance Studio	Veronica Coolgal

Special Skills

Black Belt in Aikido (3rd degree), burp on cue, walk on hands, levitation, trapeze artist, fluent in Serbian and Mandarin Chinese

Elizabeth Terrel

Your Statement of Purpose
The Statement of Purpose, if one is requested, is just another chance to tell who you are and what makes you "tick." It is a one-page document that is all about you and why you want to pursue training.

Here's how I recommend writing it:
1. Start writing. Just start. Don't over-think it before you start writing stuff down.
2. Write three to four pages about why you love acting and/or theatre, what you have to offer, why you want to do this for a living, how you see yourself contributing, what it is that especially excites you about theatre, etc.
3. Set what you've written aside for a few days.
4. Revisit your document and see what you have written that tells the most about *who you are*. Mark those parts.
5. At the same time, have someone (or multiple people) read the 3-4 page paper and mark the parts they think best represent you.
6. Create a shorter version that includes the material that is unique to you - the stuff that really says who YOU are.
7. Proofread, edit, spell-check, and edit it down to a one-page document.
8. Have multiple people proofread it for spelling, grammar, and punctuation.

The wording does not need to be extremely formal (it should sound like you) but it does need to be well written. Have someone who knows your theatrical work review it. And also have someone review it for quality of writing.

The Audition Bag

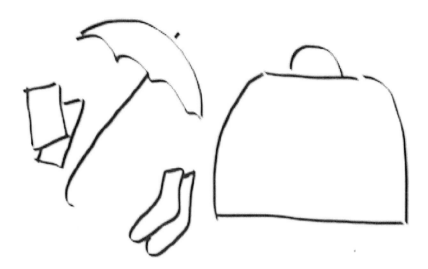

You need a bag that you take with you to auditions. It contains specific things.

These items live in your bag. That way you don't have to repack your bag all the time and you won't accidentally leave something out.

Your audition bag contains:
♦ A notebook with
    1) Headshots
    2) Resumes
    3) Your monologues, typed out, one per page
    4) Your audition sheet music if you are a singer
♦ A hairbrush or comb
♦ Hairspray

♦ A barrette that looks good with your outfit in case you cannot get your hair to stay out of your face

♦ Lip color, an eye pencil, and mascara for touchups

♦ Your audition shoes and socks, stockings, etc.

♦ An extra pair of socks, stockings, etc.

♦ Accessories for your outfit (perhaps a belt you don't want to travel in, etc.)

♦ A bottle of water that does not leak

♦ Medication for allergies, headaches, etc. if you require it

♦ Band aids

♦ A scarf to cover your head in rain/snow that won't give you "hat hair"

♦ Snack - food bar, nuts - something with nutritional value that won't spoil

♦ Toothbrush and floss

♦ Mints (better than gum because you might forget to spit out the gum)

1-13 Reward yourself

After every audition, reward yourself - now and forever, for the rest of your life.

The reward need not be extravagant or expensive. It can be a mocha drink, a walk in the park, 15 minutes to read a book you love that has no literary value, a few minutes of "silly TV", a relaxing bath, an ice cream cone, or a few minutes on the phone with a friend.

The important thing is that BEFORE the audition you decide what your reward will be and AFTER the audition you consciously shift into honoring yourself for having done the audition, and reward yourself!

You earn the reward by DOING THE AUDITION. It is not based on how well you think you did in the audition. It is earned by simply showing up and doing it. If you did an audition, you have earned a reward. Period. So enjoy it!

1-14 The training programs: what they usually do and how they usually do it

How do you know if they want you?
Generally, program auditions take place January through March. Offers are usually made mid-March to mid-April. There will be cases where you may even get an offer later. For example, you may have been "waitlisted", which means they have made offers to other people first, but you *are* on the list of people they're interested in. They may call you and accept you later because they didn't find what they were looking for or because someone turned them down.

There's no shame in being wait-listed!
What if you got an offer only because someone else turned them down?
So what????
If you want to go to the school, GO TO THE SCHOOL no matter how the offer comes. People turn down offers for a wide variety of reasons and offers are made for a wide variety of reasons.

Maybe they made the offer to someone else first because they made offers to a lot of people with light hair and that other person had dark hair, so they made the offer to the dark haired person first. It can be as simple (and as seemingly silly) as that. It does not mean you are less talented.

If a miracle happens and they make you an offer on the spot, you should not accept it on the spot unless you know that program is the one you want.

How do programs select actors?
Most programs are looking for a variety of people (or "types") in each class they accept. For example, they want one or two ingénues, a couple of people who can play older women, a "character" woman, and then the same in men. Otherwise they can't do a wide variety of plays.

How many actors will they take?
Programs accept different numbers of people. Some take 8, some take 20, some take 30, and some take more.

How long do you have to decide after they make you an offer?
Ask them how long you have to decide when they make the offer. That is a question only they can answer.

What if more than one school makes you an offer?
Then you get to decide which one you want to go to! Go and visit if at all possible. I tell people to pick the one that feels like "home" to them.

Can you videotape your audition for a program?
Read the website carefully and it will probably tell you. If it doesn't and you absolutely cannot get there for an onsite audition, call and ask.

But you should know that a live person in the room is always more interesting than a video. If the audition is for a school you really want to go to, audition in person if at all possible.

1-15 Things to know about your auditors

Most of the auditors are or were actors
We know what you're going through. We know you are scared and we understand why. And we wish you knew we don't want you to be scared, but we know you are anyway. It's just part of the process. If we had time, we'd give you a hug.

We want you to do well
We are really, really, really rooting for you!!! We want YOU to be the answer to all our recruitment and casting issues!

We see your potential
As trainers, we look for potential. We see your potential. That should make you feel great. We are not only seeing you as you are, but also as you can be.

We know whom we can train well
We know whom we can train. We recruit those people. If we don't recruit you it may simply mean that you're not a great fit for what we have to offer. It does not mean you don't have talent.

We like it when you let us see YOU
We really like it when you relax and let us see who you are. We like it when you treat us like the kind people we are - people who have chosen to work with actors because we love them and want them to succeed.

There's nothing more to say about that. We don't do this because we get paid a whole lot. We do this because we love what we do and what we do is work with actors.

We don't get many breaks
That's why we may be eating and drinking at the table. It's the only chance we get to do so.

It's always best to assume your auditors don't get breaks. Are there some rude people in the world? Yes. But most of us just didn't get a break to eat…

If you are waiting to audition and the auditors take a restroom break, that may delay your audition a bit, but ultimately it's good for you… think about it… we are now relaxed and happy.

1-16 What will you learn as a theatre major? Ten reasons to study theatre

This section is especially good for parents to read. It may also be useful for spouses and supportive others. It is written with those in mind who want to support you in your dreams but may not understand how studying theatre will help you in your life.

It is also for *you* - so you realize and continue to appreciate how valuable your arts education is.

Multiple studies have been done over the years that cite the value of an arts education and specifically the value of a theatre education. If you look, you can find many of them online. What I list here relates directly to information presented in this book.

Ten reasons to study theatre
Let's look at what we have considered in this book that will help you in your life.

1) Auditioning builds confidence. Every interview, career, and situation in life is benefitted by increased confidence.

2) Auditioning fosters the ability to enter a room bravely and put yourself and your dreams on the line. Again, this makes you better at everything you will ever do.

3) Overcoming self-consciousness through curiosity about others makes you a kinder and more interesting person.

4) Selecting and preparing pieces gives you exposure to a broad range of ideas and many different ways to look at the world. The more plays you do and the more characters you play, the more you learn about the world and the people in it. Theatre people tend to be rather open-minded for this very reason: we must learn to look at the world in ways that we wouldn't see if we only looked at it from our own demographic, our own socio-economic background, even our own gender.

5) Theatre is a collaborative art form. You will learn strong people skills and the ability to resolve, or at least live with, differences.

6) Discipline. There are few careers that require the discipline that theatre requires. Memorizing, researching, preparing scene work, showing up at odd hours to rehearse after a full day of work or classes or both - this requires *commitment* and *discipline*.

7) Work ethic. Theatre doesn't work if the people in it don't work. We show up and do our jobs out of commitment and love for our craft, and are usually getting paid very little in the beginning. Our days are long and our rehearsals are at night. Theatre artists WORK HARD - it's that simple.

8) Teamwork. In this collaborative art form, theatre artists learn to work with people who are interested in the process from a different perspective. For example, the set designer wants it to look right, the costume designer wants it to be period specific and not catch on the furniture, the lighting designer is interested in

lighting angles, the director wants the actors to be able to move across the stage in a particular way, and they are all passionate about their point of view and they all have to work together to make it successful.

From just the perspective of the actor, actors working in an ensemble work very closely together and learn to rely on one another physically and emotionally - they get good at forming close working relationships quickly.

9) Actors learn about putting one's ego on the back burner. Because of the celebrity that sometimes accompanies fame in the acting world, there seems to be a notion that actors have huge egos. This is rarely true. Actors set aside their own agendas and embody characters that are not them, they often do jobs for little or no money because there is a story worth telling, they learn to accept differences of opinion regarding their work, and they do what it takes to get the show up. Actors who cannot do these things just don't work in the long run. Because of the competitive nature of the industry and the difficulty of putting themselves and their dreams on the line in auditions, actors develop a healthy sense of self and a determination that could be interpreted as ego. But this sense of self is very different from the egotism that those outside the business seem to expect actors to possess.

10) The ability to present oneself in a professional manner is something you are doing in preparation for

auditioning. This will serve you in practically every aspect of your life.

Part 2

Interviews: Undergraduate Training Programs

The interviews you are about to read were conducted verbally, recorded, and transcribed. Interviewees are all working professionals who conduct auditions for acting training programs that admit/accept students based on auditions. They are all experienced auditors and recruit for some of the best training programs in the country.

Keep in mind when reading, that these interviews were conducted verbally and transcribed. There is an informal quality to the answers that makes them imminently readable. You may find it helpful and entertaining to read them out loud. These are really conversations, with my questions (and occasional comments) in bold type. The questions I asked are questions frequently asked by auditionees. You will find the material covered varies slightly from person to person, depending on what the interviewees especially wanted to talk about.

Because of the nature of graduate acting training programs, those who audition candidates for graduate school tend to be looking for a more specific type of student, depending on the type of program they have. The interviews with graduate program auditors can be found in Part 4, as the specific information is useful, but may be slightly overwhelming if you're just starting to figure this whole audition thing out! I'm not saying don't read those interviews, but maybe wait a while. The interviewees are still delightful, kind people, but if you're auditioning for an undergraduate or similar program (like an internship or another type of training program) I would rather you didn't have the specificity of the graduate training auditions on your mind.

Enjoy these interviews! Spoiler alert: in most cases you will find the information shared by the auditors supports the information in Part 1. I think it's particularly valuable for you to have the opportunity to read advice in other voices. (And by the way, I did not select people who agreed with me. Nor did I edit the interviews so they supported Part 1. I'm not that crafty.)

You will notice that there are some minor discrepancies between auditors. This is largely because they audition actors for their specific programs, and different programs have different strengths and different ways of training actors, as well as different focuses.

Lastly, the purpose of these interviews is not for you to craft your audition to fit any particular program or auditor. Many of the auditors actually addressed the futility of such an attempt. The purpose of these interviews is to give you an opportunity to hear about auditioning from a variety of auditors who select actors for a wide variety of programs. I will say, however, that you may recognize programs or people who especially appeal to you - good! All programs are not the same! This is a good example of how important it is for you to pay attention when auditioning - be curious about the person behind the table and the program they represent. You are assessing them, too!

2-1 Cynthia Bassham
University of California, Irvine
Head of Undergraduate Acting
Lecturer SOE

UCI Audition format: 2 minutes total, 2 pieces. 2 ½ minutes if the person auditioning also sings

What do you look for in an audition?
I am looking for a moment of *living*. Is there a telltale sign of their humanity? It's as simple as that really - can they live and breathe while helping tell a story? Because it's not 'can you memorize and stand in front of us' - it's not about that. It is nice if there is a sense of command of the room and an invitation to take up space and for us to take up space with them, but it doesn't have to be spectacular.

We're NOT looking for bravado. We're not looking for artificial theatricality. I should clarify that: Robert Cohen was always looking for theatricality, meaning allowing yourself to meet the character and to give it its full weight, whatever that might be. Can you LIVE in the given circumstances? Can you meet the character where they are?

I find a lot of actors, and myself included when I was younger... well, I felt like I had to show EVERYTHING I could do. I thought I had to show the kitchen sink every time because perhaps you might not know that I'm capable of XYZ and I needed to prove it. I needed to show you my A-Z in my 2 minutes. And there's just no way!

An audition is like your calling card. Throughout your life you'll throw out a lot of calling cards. And they don't have a lot of weight. And they don't have a lot of size. And it's a simple gesture. It's just [tossing down a card motion] "Hey - this is me," "This is me again," "Hi! This is me," "Hi again, this is me."

You have to be a little careful about the material you pick. Because quite often what happens is you're trying to show that you can stretch yourself. But if you do "fuckin' Ruthie, fuckin' Ruthie" and we get bombarded with a whole bunch of "fuck you, fuck you" audition pieces, I can get WEARY as the auditor. I don't want to hear scatological, I don't want to hear cursing, I don't want to hear degrading women, I don't want to hear hate speech. You may think that those things are exciting and edgy and "I'll give you what I got," but it DOES tip a hand that you may not be aware of, and I may form some opinions about *you* based on the material you pick. And so you need to be a little cautious.

I think it's important to talk to whoever's your mentor to get feedback on your audition.

Keep in mind that 'contrasting pieces' doesn't necessarily mean 'happy' and 'sad.' There are lots of ways to contrast. In addition to mood, you need to think about what other ways they contrast. Do they have different energy and different focus? So it's not just about tragedy versus comedy - it's about can you live in a different space and can I watch you do that?

Always do two pieces. ALWAYS do two pieces. If you sing, the song you do should be contrasting as well - the song is an audition piece as well. It's not enough to just show off that you can sing. Have that be a part of the spectrum of what it is that you're able to do well. Have it be different from the other things. If you just did a heart-felt piece and then you do a romantic song, what's that telling me that's new about who you are?

Also, be passionate about what you pick, because you're going to be with it for the long haul. Love it, love it, love it. And be willing to go many, many different directions with it. Because that's part of the process. Don't get married to the way you shape a piece, because quite often the people that you audition for will want to see how you take direction, so be willing to throw [the way you perform your piece] out at the drop of a hat. You might even want to practice that with your coach if you have one - practice "now do it as a time-step," "now do it as Ethel Merman," whatever it is - just try it in many different ways.

What is the ideal audition outfit? You can also answer that with what you do not want to see.
I get so tired of cute little women in short little skirts with shoes that are five miles high. Snore, snore, snore. Women, put some thought into what the pieces are that you're doing. If you're playing a britches role, do you want to be wearing a skirt? If you're Rosalind saying, "What shall I do with my doublet and hose?" do you want to have a skirt on? You want to wear something that supports you but is not a costume. I think it's useful if you're playing something that's a little manly to wear a long pantsuit that's a little flowing - that feels skirt-like, that could be skirt-like, but that isn't a skirt.

Be careful of patterns. If your clothes are too busy then I begin to look at your clothes and not at you. That's true across the board, for men and women.

I want you to look nice, but I don't want you to look like you went out this morning and bought your outfit. I want you to be comfortable in it. And I want it to be so there's nothing binding in the least, and yet it is form-fitting enough so that I can get a sense of your basic shape. I don't want you to wear a muumuu - yes, you'd be really comfortable in that, but that won't tell me anything about how you move and how you look.

I like bright colors, but not too bright. Jewel tones are pretty awesome - like a rich ruby or rich turquoise - things that pop. Black slacks. Things that are classic. This is not necessarily your opportunity to make a fashion statement. If you like wearing Doc Martens along with your A-line skirt, maybe this isn't the opportunity for that. Be you, be comfortable, and don't be too distracting.

What I don't like are guys that haven't made the effort to dress up a bit. I don't mind sneakers, but if you're wearing the ones that are beginning to come apart you need to step up your game a little bit. If you're more comfortable in sneakers than dress shoes I'm absolutely fine with that, but make sure they're your nice pair.

Is there anything that you would like to add?
Control the things you can control and let go of the things you don't have control over.

Remember that what you're doing is offering a gift. For the brief little time that you have. Yes, people are weighing you in the balance, but you have no control over that. That's actually why you're there. That's actually what you want them to be doing. They WANT to love you. And what you are offering to them is a gift.

And in the moment before you say your name, in the breath that you take in before you launch into a whole bunch of talking, make sure you land those moments for yourself so that you feel like you experience them in a way that's meaningful for you.

2-2 Jim Daniels
University of Texas at Austin
Senior Lecturer in Acting

How many students do you accept into the program each year?
14 to 16.

How many students do you audition each year?
700 to 900.

When an auditionee walks into the room, what are you looking for?
There is a certain (almost indefinable) stage presence and energy, and you have the thought, "might we not want to party with this person?"

Other qualities that are present when I see a good audition:

There is a sense that they're actually talking to the other person, trying to affect the other person, trying to change the other person [the Imaginary Other], that the energy is all outer-directed, towards the other person.

Also, how physical they are, how well you can hear them – those things are indicators that they might be stage material.

A sense of humor and imagination is important.

Sometimes they just have the ability to make choices that come from out of left field, or that surprise you, that may seem like oddball choices, but they make perfect sense - they just aren't choices I would've thought of.

The other thing is that there's just a simplicity, just an honesty, a feeling that they are telling the truth. We are looking to see something of the person revealed through the work. They open their mouths, and you sit there and think, "Oh, she's experienced that. She knows what she's talking about." There's a sense of authenticity, truthfulness in what they're doing… Sometimes it comes from a wisdom or a savvy that's beyond their years.

How long is the ideal monologue?
One minute or less each with the auditions we go to.

Do you expect to hear Shakespeare?
No, I don't expect to. I tend to advise against it because there's generally just not a lot of experience dealing with it. Although every once in a while a student will surprise you, and it's obvious they're very literate. They are very solid with language, they really understand the thoughts and the journey of the character, and they are connected to what they're saying. Every once in a while there's somebody who seems really at home with it. Sometimes it's from a really adept high school teacher and sometimes the student is just incredibly talented and they just "get it."

Are there monologues or types of monologues that you absolutely never want to hear again?
If you had asked me during the audition season I could have named some specific ones perhaps. We do see a lot of redundancy, and may see five or six of the same monologue, but I work to stay open to it because one person *delivers.* And then it's good that I didn't shut myself down from hearing that same monologue again, because when they do it it's like, "Oh my God, I've never heard that monologue!" and yet I've seen five of them that day.

I never think Christopher Durang works very well. It's hard to make it work.

A lot of what we do see, unfortunately, is totally unheard of plays with really poor material. Auditionees haven't been advised well or they come from a school with no program and they are just pulling it together by the skin of their teeth. So we see cases in which the material they pick is really third rate material. We don't want phony or melodramatic monologues or phony or caricature-y type pieces, or pieces that are more like stand-up comedy routines.

Do you have any pet peeves at auditions that you want to share?
Sloppy dress irritates me, but I often get the impression that it's not so much an act of rebellion or thumbing their noses at the process - in a lot of cases they just don't seem to know any better. Some folks, God bless them, they just don't know any better.

There will be guys who come in a suit and tie and there's something about it that looks way too formal.

Some of the women come in what looks like high heels and cocktail dresses and it's not appropriate and I have to kind of close my eyes to it because it could be just a dumb choice and they're actually very talented.

And then some auditionees just look like they couldn't care less, and there's not a sense of respect for the occasion. Some of it just seems to be the style - everything is kind of jeans and T-shirts and it's seems like there's sometimes a school of thought that it's not a special occasion, so you just show up wearing whatever you're wearing.

We've seen a lot of people wearing layer after layer after layer of stuff - scarves and heavy jewelry and vests - and I just think they should take half of that stuff off, because we can't see what they look like!

Well you just answered the next question, which is 'What is the ideal thing to wear to an audition?' Is there anything you'd like to add?
The most effective guys tend to wear khakis and button downs and hard-soled shoes. And for girls it seems to be most effective if they keep it clean and simple - like slacks and a top or a dress that doesn't call too much attention to itself. In all cases they should be able to move well.

Anything else that you would like to add? Anything you think they need to know?
I always like it when they take that moment just to say good morning or good afternoon and introduce themselves. And then when they say thank you at the end of the audition. I think one of my pet peeves is when they do an introduction and they maybe do something cutesy to call attention to themselves instead of using that time to connect with us behind the table.

A lot of times you can tell just in the way they introduce themselves or say thank you at the end of the audition that they are sincere and present and not just doing some routine thing they know they are supposed to say. It seems like a tiny thing, but I have actually heard a colleague say something to the effect of "if their audition had been as honest as their introduction was, I would have been more engaged."

One of my pet peeves is when they blow through their introduction – their name and the names of their pieces - so fast that I don't know who they are or what they're doing. I find myself spending time making sure I've got their name right, rather than being able to watch their audition. If they talk too fast I spend time thinking "what did they say? what is this from?" Clarity in your name and the pieces you're doing is incredibly helpful.

It is also disturbing when people come in and introduce themselves and just the way they stand there is so self-effacing and so low energy that I start to write them off. But then when they do their monologue there may be energy and presence there! That always leaves me thinking, "Why didn't you bring as much energy to your introduction and name as you did to your pieces?"
Don't throw your own name away!

When we have them audition in-house in Austin we have a chance to talk to them and interview them more extensively. I'm always fascinated when, in talking to them, I find them to be very mature, very smart, very intelligent, they have other interests, they're easy to engage, they ask questions. And again there is the life energy that, regardless of how their audition went... well, there are students that we called back just on a hunch. And in the interview they are incredibly interesting people, and we want them in our student body. We want them to be a part of the program just because they are smart, intelligent, engaging human beings. And we sometimes think, "Okay, we'll work a little harder with them to teach them to act" - and its worth it, because they're great people! So their ability to just be present and open in an interview situation is really important. It carries a lot of weight.

Have you ever seen the handout from Syracuse University, "What Theatre Majors Learn" by Louis E. Catron? It's about 25 things you learn by being a theatre major. It includes a lot of things about leadership, decision-making, cooperation, working with authority, time management, and stuff like that. I give it to all of my students.

When I talk to the parents, one of the things that we talk about when it comes to being a theatre major is that, yes, we all hope they get rich and famous. But the ultimate goal of being a theatre major is to learn to be a better person. To learn to be a better person by learning to listen to people, to learn to tell the truth, to learn to problem solve, to be engaged in relationship.

Maybe I've told you this story, but a few years ago I was talking to an acquaintance and he was talking about this one actor whom he said was an incredible actor - absolutely a brilliant, great actor. And he went on to become a firefighter in Portland, Oregon. And my friend said, "But I'll tell you this, he's the *best* firefighter in Portland, Oregon!" Meaning that's the kind of guy he was. These skills we teach them – yes, you hope they become successful - but what we're really teaching them is to be the bigger, better person. And that's what will serve them no matter what they ultimately do professionally.

Whenever I get a chance to talk to parents I say, "Listen, we know you're scared stiff about your student being a theatre major. I know you wonder how that will work. But this is the bigger picture that you have to trust in: We are focused on them becoming better people."

2-3 Stanton Davis
Northern Illinois University
Head of BFA Performance
Head of Voice & Speech

What are you looking for when an auditionee comes into the room?
First: eye contact. A willingness to engage authentically when they first come in the room so that we get the sense that they're not forcing us into that artificial role of auditor and auditionee, but that they're capable of carrying on authentic communication. Meaning communicating authentically instead of forcing us into that artificial relationship, which auditioning is. That's really it, when they first come in the room.

There's something I think they often don't get, which is that the audition begins the moment we see them. Even out in the hall. And that's really important, because for example, my assistants see people before I do and often times they may come in and say, "okay here's your next person – quite an attitude" or "here's your next person – they're a sweetheart" or "here's your next person – their mom's out there brow-beating them." I get from them what's happening in the hall - the moment that they make contact with the school, their audition begins.

That's something that they really need to understand: If I'm trying to decide on whether a person is for us, because I'm leery of something I've seen, I will ask my assistants how they were outside. So they need to know that that's important.

How long is the ideal monologue?
1 minute and 20 seconds.

What is your audition format?
We ask for two monologues, not to exceed two minutes each. Rarely do we see the full 2 minutes of a monologue.

If you cut them off, does it mean anything bad?
No. Actually, sometimes I'm cutting them off because I've seen what I need to see and I want to move on to working on something that I need to see if they can do. I've seen enough in the piece to know what they're capable of; I just need to ask them for specific stuff. I work pieces extensively.

Do you expect to hear Shakespeare?

No, but I'd like to hear something that shows they can handle more complicated text. It doesn't have to be Shakespeare – it could be Chekhov, it could be George Bernard Shaw, or even something more contemporary like *Marat Sade* or something along those lines. Even things like Bertoldt Brecht - in which the text is complicated and the language is somewhat heightened. I like to be able to see if they can handle that because our program specializes in that. But if they don't, it's not a mark against them; it just doesn't show that they have that particular skill set. If they're comfortable with it, they *should* do something like that [heightened text], but it doesn't need to be Shakespeare. I think Shakespeare is harder than some of these other playwrights and I don't want them to do Shakespeare unless they're super confident. If they are, then by all means, do it. I've seen some amazing Shakespeare pieces from students, but they shouldn't do them unless they're ready to rock our socks.

What monologues do you never want to hear again?

Helena from *Midsummer Night's Dream*: "Through Athens I am thought as fair as she..."
Viola from *Twelfth Night*: "I left no ring with her..."
I think I never want to see anything by Nicky Silver ever again in an audition. Or Neil LaBute. I think that both of them are trivial and they bely a sort of trivial nature in the person that would choose them, and I think Neil LaBute stuff is just negative and mean, and when people speak that text it does not sell them well because the *material* is so negative and mean. So I would just never want to see anything by those two playwrights.

Christopher Durang is questionable because a lot of it's cutesy and it's hard to discover whether the actor can go deep with just cutesy.

So any monologue that shows them off in a "this is funny and cutesy" sort of way is a poor choice. I would rather they'd find something in *Equus* or *Royal Hunt of The Sun God* – something where there's a really funny moment in a really deep piece, like something by Peter Schaffer. And there are funny moments in monologues that otherwise show off different qualities. If your whole monologue is to get one cheap laugh, you shouldn't do it.

How many auditionees do you see each year?
500.

How many do you accept each year?
We accept 20.

What is your pet peeve at auditions?
Neil LaBute. (laughter) Also, I can't stand it when people shout. That strong, righteous indignation quality that people play that's not an *emotion*, it's an emotional *quality* - where they're playing the strong, outraged, wronged [character]. I fear that more women fall into this than men, but it's this "now I'm going to lecture you" quality. The thing is as an auditor the last thing I want is 20 monologues where people are lecturing, essentially, *me*.

Also, people that stand there frozen solid – that's horrible. I don't want them standing like a man at the block waiting to be shot!

When I'm engaging them in conversation and they tune me out – they aren't listening or engaging with me – that's a no go. Because if they can't have a conversation and stay present with me for 15 minutes after we've had an audition, they're not gonna do it for four years.

What is the ideal audition outfit?
That's a really good question.
I see people come in in suits sometimes. I think that's too much. I think it should be upscale casual – it shouldn't be all the way to formal.

I would say, nothing that constricts too much. I do want to see them move.

There are things, for example, that women sometimes wear that are inappropriate. If you're 17 or 18, don't be dressing hootchie-cootchie: dresses that are too short, tops that are cut too low, see-through blouses - anything like that makes me feel like, "no, I don't need to see that." And it also belies a lack of trust in themselves.

Watch out for too-high heels for women.

Avoid distracting jewelry like huge earrings. No facial jewelry – take that stuff out. Tongue studs – don't audition with a tongue stud. You can't articulate. Besides, it's just creepy (laughs). I know it's hip for young people, but for a lot of us older folks it's just creepy! And I'm thinking that if I feel that way, a lot of other auditors, many of whom are much older than me, are going to have that same reaction.

I don't like hair that is in their face so I can't see their face.

I also think on guys it's best if they're not wearing tennis shoes – it's better if they're wearing a leather shoe.

They should wear something that they could wear in an office, but that they can move in.

Do you want to hear singing for an acting major?
Absolutely. I often ask if they have a song – even acapella. It gives me some idea what their voice can do. I'm a voice teacher, too, and that's a voice I'm going to be working with for four years. Regardless of whether or not they can sing well, being able to hear them sing is a big deal.

Is there anything else you'd like to add?
Yeah! I think a lot of kids think that a really well-coached slick monologue is what we're looking for, and what I'm looking for is the raw material: trainability, a sense of spirit.

I want to get a sense of who they are as an artist and what they care about, and that's reflected in the pieces they choose, the depth of their understanding of those pieces, and if I talk with them about one of their pieces I want them to be conversant in it. I'm looking for people who are interested in this as an art form, and as such they should have some excitement about what they're doing in the room. Don't pick these pieces from monologue books where they don't know who the character is. Pick a piece of good literature, know the playwright, be excited about the material that you're choosing so that if the auditor has a conversation with you about it you can be conversant about it. And enthusiastic! I think it's the enthusiasm that gets me, because we're going to spend four years with somebody and we choose those people carefully because if we don't we're stuck with a person we aren't interested in for four years! So we're not just looking for a skillfully crafted monologue, we're looking for *people*. So the more you can do to make sure that when you walk in the room you show us who you really are, the better. Because we'll train you. We'll train the actor, but we can't train the spirit. The *spirit* – that's what you need to bring in on your own.

Conversation including assistants Bethany Mangum and Emily Reider:
Emily: Something I've learned from working this side of the table is that a thank you note goes a long way. It means a lot when a candidate lets us know they're interested in *us*.
Stanton: They go right to the top of our list.
Returning people's calls promptly is also really important. When we make offers, the ones we liked a lot who have been in contact with us are the first ones we make offers to.
Bethany: Also, it's important for them to know that once they're in the room, the audition is *theirs*. Don't feel any pressure from the parent outside the room – go in and just own who you are inside the room. They can just *be there*, and they're enough. It's their time!

Stanton: And one last thing, they need to remember to *breathe*. There are so many that literally hold their breath when they're in the room, and when you valve off your breath you're valving off emotion, too. So they can't be completely emotionally available in their pieces if they're not breathing. So right before you launch into any of your pieces, take a big, deep breath and then go into it. Remember to do this fundamentally human thing. Take a breath.

2-4 Dwandra Lampkin
Western Michigan University
Associate Professor of Acting
Director of Multicultural Theatre
Formerly at Ball State, Assistant Professor of Acting (8 years)

Audition requirements: Two 1-minute monologues, contrasting

What are you looking for when an auditionee walks into the room?
The first thing I'm looking for is a sense of "confidence." Not necessarily the kind that says, "I believe in my abilities" - although that's great to have - but instead the kind that says, "This audition room is exactly where I'm supposed to be at this moment and I am going to seize

this opportunity to the best of my ability." That's the first thing that I look for.

In terms of the actual audition, I want to be able to detect that an actor has actually spent a least some time preparing for the audition. If I get the sense that they're walking in ill prepared I'm probably going to shut down right away. I can usually decipher the difference between someone whose nerves get in the way, versus someone who comes in clueless in terms of what's going on. I find myself wanting to say, "You didn't spend *any* time on this did you?" I'm not open to that at all.

What monologues or types of monologues do you never want to hear again?
I'm not crazy about monologues that have excessive use of the "n-word" in them. We cut monologues to fit time constraints, there's no reason why we shouldn't cut words within those monologues to avoid unnecessary distractions from the piece itself. In the context of an *entire play*, i.e. a monologue from an August Wilson play, the excessive use of the "n-word" works (well most of the time anyway.) However, when taken out of the context of the play, and when given a small window in which to perform, it can be a bit much. It's like, "Ok enough already, I get the point!" The same goes for excessive cursing, if you're slinging the f-bomb around a million times in one monologue, where is there room for the story?

As far as females are concerned I don't like to see a lot of victim-y monologues. The whole "woe is me - he broke my heart" pieces. I agree that we go through many things, but we don't always need to be the victim in the story that we're telling, specifically when it comes to an audition. I'm not saying that women can't show vulnerability, as a matter of fact I think those are some of the more interesting stories; what I am saying is find pieces that have a sense of balance in them. "You broke my heart, I cried for a week, my tear ducts are dry and now I'm finally going to start that business that I've been talking about for years. Oh, and what was your name again?" I want to see more of *those* pieces.

Do you want to hear Shakespeare for undergraduate actor auditions?
Personally, I prefer not to hear it, especially from young actors who don't have a clear understanding of it yet. I don't think they should even attempt it; it's like learning to speak a new language - just because you can say "bonjour" and "au revoir" doesn't mean you know how to speak French. Shakespeare takes time and practice, using an undergraduate audition as a practice ground wouldn't be the wisest choice. I'll be able to assess more of who you are in something more contemporary.

What is the ideal audition outfit?
Let's see…well for guys it's simple, I like to see that they actually ironed their clothes; it shows me that you actually care enough to put some thought into what you looked like. Jeans I'm fine with, no holes in them. Dress pants are acceptable as long as you're comfortable in them, but don't wear a full suit unless the role calls for it in some form or another. Oh, and this might seem obvious, but make sure your clothes are clean, or at least have the appearance of being clean. There's nothing worse than

seeing an actor walk into an audition room with multiple stains spattered all over his clothes. Ugh!

Women, I always say if you can't walk in a pair of shoes, don't wear them. I don't like seeing women walk into an audition room with high heels on, and by high I mean 3 inches or more. They give a false sense of your physical truth, they make annoying 'clicking' sounds when you walk into and around the room, and they don't allow you to be grounded within the rehearsal space. Now, there are always exceptions to these 'rules,' if high heels lend to a character's traits, then by all means wear those high heels, but more times than not you really should leave them at home.

I'm also not a fan of clothes that show off a lot of cleavage - it's your *work* that I want to see, not your breasts. If your breasts are up for a role then that's an entirely different audition, and I'm not casting that show. The truth of the matter is it doesn't even have to be linked to sexuality; the fact is that where there is cleavage, often eyes will follow. Don't allow that to be a distraction from your audition even for a moment. Choose your clothes wisely.

Lastly, don't wear a bunch of crazy colors to the point where my eyes are hurting just to look at you. Keep it simple, know the colors that are flattering on you, and dress comfortably.

2-5 Tanera Marshall
University of Illinois at Chicago
Associate Professor of Theatre

You recruit for which programs?
I recruit for the *BFA in Acting* program and for the *BA in Theatre & Performance*. Both require an audition.

What is your general audition format?
We ask for two contrasting monologues which we have them do right away. We also warm them up five or six at a time before the audition. After their monologues, students sit and chat with us for a few minutes.

I suppose it would be helpful for prospective students to know that sometimes they may go blank or perhaps something interesting or unusual happens by accident in their audition, and then we might invite them to play make-believe in an improvisational way. We may say, "Do you write poetry? Do you want to sing a song? Would you like to have a tea party? Can you tell us a story?" It is a chance for them to do something else that's playful that reveals their sense of imagination and ability to "play make-believe." We offer this as a way of taking the pressure *off* of them, rather than applying pressure! It's a chance for really creative people to show us their creativity in other ways. In most cases, though, the audition format is pretty traditional in the sense that we do a quick group warm-up, hear two monologues, and follow up with a brief interview.

How long is the ideal monologue?
Two minutes or less per monologue.

Are there any monologues or types of monologues that you simply never want to hear again?
(Laughs) Sure. No monologues off the Internet. There's not anything inherently wrong with the Internet, but a monologue that was simply written for a collection or web site lacks context - it isn't part of a larger story arc - and therefore lacks dramatic tension, usually.

It's funny... I imagine there are people who are sick of this or that monologue. I don't have that issue. When a monologue is done well, it's like hearing it for the first time anyway, right? So I find I'm not prejudiced against *particular* monologues, I'm prejudiced against *bad* [poorly written] monologues. Which are defined for me by what I just mentioned: things that lack dramatic tension; things that lack a clear objective for the person speaking.

Choosing a monologue is so important. It has to be well written, and it has to suit the actor.

What is the ideal audition outfit?
I think something that is comfortable: so not too tight, not too short. Be prepared to move. Nice slacks, a nice top, sensible shoes. Perhaps young people want to come across as youthful and attractive, but they should be sensible about being dressed for anything that may come up in the audition. They may be asked to move at the last minute, for instance. They may be asked to do their piece standing on their head, or standing on a chair...
Literally on their head?
No.

Okay. I just wanted to specify that so that they wouldn't be freaked out. ☺

When your "ideal candidate" walks into the room, what is it you're looking for? What do you see?
I'm interested in somebody who is self-possessed, by which I mean they reflect a sense of comfort, ease with oneself. It's OK to be nervous though. (Smiles) You don't have to not be nervous.

We like someone who is clear about why they're there and what they want. When asked why they're interested in our program a lot of prospective students say things like, "I really love Chicago." And that has nothing to do *really* with our program, but they chose to audition for *our* program. So a sense of purpose in selecting programs is important.

Probably the most important thing is a sense of playfulness. When you don't have a lot of skills, and you haven't been studying acting yet, *that's fine!* We don't want someone necessarily who has had a lot of experience; rather, we want somebody who has that *spark*, that fire for playing make-believe, and enjoying themselves in "never never land"…in front of other people. If you can *play*, you're more likely to get in. (Smiles)

Would you like to add anything else about the ideal candidate for your program?
Our program is on the smaller side. And therefore we are close with each other. Knowing what a small family we are, we are very careful about selecting people who clearly can play well with others. I like to say that we don't have divas; we don't have *room* for divas. There are certainly a lot of divas who are enormously talented who will do well in another program, and who may succeed as professional performers, but if we sense that the personality mix isn't right for our students - who are quite unpretentious and yet very focused - we may pass on that person.

Is there anything that you would like to add? Anything that makes you think, "Oh I want people auditioning to know this"?
Yes. It's not about getting it all perfect. It's not about perfection in any sense. There is no perfect. But to be *prepared* is good. So… preparation involves rehearsal and timing your monologues so that you know they come in under two minutes or whatever is being asked. But that doesn't mean in the moment you can't be a human being

and mess up. It's OK to mess up! To go back and start again, perhaps. Or we will work with you and will find some other way to get your creativity to come out. It's funny - we often see people who are really polished and have no spark, or people that have a lot of spark and haven't ever really rehearsed their monologues before. So they are really unprepared.

So you're looking for the prepared person who still has a spark - who hasn't worked and rehearsed the spark out of their monologue?
That's a great way of putting it. Yes. You can quote yourself on that! ☺

Be prepared, but you don't have to be perfect! Be prepared: ready for anything and everything. But the spark... the twinkle in the eye... it has to be there!

2-6 Tamara Meneghini
Department of Theatre & Dance, University of Colorado Boulder
Associate Professor

When an auditionee walks into the room what are you hoping to see? What are you looking for in that first encounter?
I am looking for *ease*. I am looking for someone who has a sense of ease walking into the room. First and foremost I am looking for somebody who can just be *present*.

How long is the ideal monologue?
For me, I usually know what I need to know in 30 seconds. However, we do a three-minute total audition time, and they can split up the time however they want.

Do you specify asking for two contrasting pieces?
Yes. We ask for two contrasting pieces that are right for them. And they can decide how they contrast. We don't specify classical, contemporary, or anything like that.

Do you expect to hear Shakespeare?
I love to hear Shakespeare. I don't know if I expect it but we hear it a lot, because we have a big classical component in our training. We have an affiliation with Colorado Shakespeare Festival. And in the program they have an entire semester of Shakespeare and an entire semester of Period Style work. So the students auditioning kind of come into the process being interested in it. And maybe they have no facility whatsoever for Shakespeare yet, but they're interested in it and maybe try it. And I always appreciate it when they do try.

Are there any monologues or types of monologues you never want to hear again?
What I don't like so much is when they do monologues that are clearly out of their age and experience range. And they are clearly doing some monologues for shock value.

I really appreciate when they've taken the time to find monologues that are really right for them or monologues that they can really connect to.
I appreciate it when they really do their homework and find things that are really right for them.

How many students do you take into the BFA acting program each year?
Between 16 and 20.

Do you have any pet peeves at auditions other than people doing material that is inappropriate for them?
What I can't stand is apologizing.

What does that mean?
"I'm sorry I didn't have this material" or "I'm sorry that I'm not ready with such and such." I really can't stand it when they apologize in the audition. And whether they verbally apologize or whether they do it with their bodies, it's just a bad thing to do.

I don't like it when they don't "hold the space" before they start. I like it when they take a moment before they start.

So you're saying that you'd like just a moment of themselves before they began?
Yes.

I like it when they say "hi" to us and acknowledge us.

I *like* to see how they can utilize space. I *really* like that and I think it's really important. So I don't prefer when they choose two pieces where they're just standing still. I like feet - I like to see feet moving and bodies moving, and I like to see how they move in their bodies. So in at least one of their pieces I'd like to see if they're comfortable in their body, not just comfortable in a chair, but I'd like to see them moving around. Not just for the sake of movement, but for the sake of my being able to see how they move in their body.

What is the ideal audition outfit?
Something that's right for them. We've been taking our students to showcase for the last three years and I teach a lot about this because... Prior to beginning the New York showcase I thought that dressing up was what they were supposed to do. But what I've learned is that what

they really need to do is dress in their sense of style. It needs to look nice but it has to be them! So if it's a woman who never wears a dress and she's trying to get herself into a dress and heels just for the sake of looking that way for the audition it's not good. It has to be them - it has to speak to who they are. Not a T-shirt and jeans, but maybe a T-shirt and jeans and a jacket for a guy. The thing now is that it has to speak to who they are and not be sloppy.

Who is the ideal candidate for your program?
We tend to accept actors that are really grounded. By that I mean they are not necessarily the most talented and skilled bunch when they come in. What's important for us is that they "play well with others." The first class they take together as a group is Building An Ensemble. We believe really firmly in teaching people to be key ensemble players. So our audition process consists of their performance of their monologues, writing an essay about why they want to be in the program, and then they also do a voice and movement component of the audition that is largely group work so that we can witness how they work and how they play together.

Is there anything you want to add that you think auditioning students should know?
When *you* are auditioning you are also auditioning *them*. I think a lot of students forget that. And I don't mean you're auditioning them [the people behind the table] in a combative or confrontive way, but the more open and available and present you can be the easier it is for you to get a sense of the energy in the room and get to know the people [behind the table]. So I always encourage

them to treat it as if the audition is giving a gift of themselves and in return they are making themselves available to perceive what we offer in the room.

As I teach the showcase class one of the things that I've discovered I'm spending a lot of time on is shifting their perception so that they learn that they have some control over the auditioning situation as well. They may discover through the audition process that it [a particular job or school] might not be the right match for them. This means they must be open and available and not spending so much time thinking about how they're going to be judged.

The other thing you learn as you get a little bit longer in the tooth or as you just get out there auditioning (and at times you're auditioning more than you're performing) is you learn to see auditioning as an opportunity to craft your own little showcase of you. Ideally it's a showcase of who you *are*, rather than who you *want to be*.

2-7 Jeff Morrison
Marymount Manhattan College
Voice & Speech, Coach

Students accepted in program each audition year: BFA 50-60
Total number auditioned annually: at least 1000
Auditions are conducted on-site during 5 weekends per year, November - March
Several off-site auditions are conducted around the country

What are your audition requirements?
One 2-minute monologue.

Do you want auditionees for the actor training program to sing?
No. Not necessary.

Do you want classics? Or do you prefer contemporary?
We want contemporary. The reason behind this is because unless... I don't want this to sound condescending, but most of the time a high school student doing classical material lacks the training and experience to deal with the reality of the complex text in a classical piece that's going to show them off in a way that we can actually tell anything about what they're doing. We can tell from a contemporary piece whether or not someone kind of has an instinct for language.

The guy that I audition with, Richard Niles, is an acting professor. The way we do the auditions is we have an acting teacher and a voice teacher in each audition. What he (Richard Niles) says is that we're looking for potential. We're not looking for them to be "*good*" - if they were "*good*" they wouldn't need to come to school. And I've seen a couple people that we've auditioned, one girl in particular, and she was already really *good*. And she didn't complete the program. And right now she's on TV. But she showed up and she auditioned and we took her, but I can remember thinking, "I don't know...what can we really teach her?" So evidently there was some other thing, probably things from her parents, pushing her to do that. Okay, so I'm getting a little off-track.

What monologues do you never want to see again?
I don't know the names of every single one...
Little Miss Firecracker
Star Spangled Girl - "I've tried to be friendly, I've tried to be cordial..."

The ozone monologue from *Angels in America* - This is my personal pet peeve because there's nothing going ON in the monologue. It's contemplative, it's very passive, and it's at the end of the play. The only reason that it resonates and works is if you've sat through five hours of *Angels in America* before you get to the monologue. I can't stand it and it fails every time.

The other things that I've seen that don't work are things from *Woyzeck* and *No Exit*. As much as I love those plays, we are a training program for young people to become successful actors with a career. What we're looking for is things like being able to breathe, being able to access yourself, being simple, playing an action. I've done a lot of experimental theatre so I sort of get the desire to do something different, but it's not appropriate for an audition in this program.

What is the ideal acting candidate for you? What are you looking for?

Someone who is honest, first of all. In other words, doesn't pretend they're not nervous. But who is nevertheless capable of actually doing something. We work with students at auditions - we basically teach an acting class and we workshop everyone's monologue. We are looking for someone who can take direction, who can try stuff even if they don't understand what's going on. What we're looking for I think is - well it's difficult to articulate - I want to say "you know it when you see it" but what we're looking for is someone who can be pretty simple and direct and inhabit imaginary circumstances in a way that we understand what the story is and who they're talking to, and we understand the importance of whatever it is that they're saying, and we understand and feel what they want. What that looks like is sometimes hard to articulate. What that means is you're not *acting at* something. It's not a question of overdoing it or not overdoing it, but are you kind of illustrating an emotion (bad) or are you feeling your way into what it might actually be like to be in that situation and then speaking out of that imaginary circumstance (good)?

What my acting colleague often does is just get people to simplify: Whom are you talking to? What do you want? He tries things to get them away from the manufactured emotional intensity of what they are doing.

As the voice person, I often work on people wandering. I root the feet and try to take all that energy and put it into the breath and voice.

What we're really looking for, I guess, to put it in a nutshell, is not someone who can audition well, but someone who can be present and make a change. Because what we are looking for is someone who has potential; who is teachable. So if someone comes in and we see a seed of something interesting and we work and work and work and nothing changes, that person is not getting in. But someone who might be yelling at the top of his lungs and might be really pumping all this fake emotion and it's terrible, and you say, "ok, let's simplify" and then there's a big change and we see something REAL, that person's getting in.

I don't know how many places run auditions like this. At [some other schools] you do your thing and they say "thank you" and it's like a professional audition. Our philosophy is that they're auditioning us as much as we're auditioning them. They are auditioning at more than one school, so we want them to get some information about two full-time faculty members: How do we think? How do we work? What is class going to feel like if you go here?

What is the ideal audition outfit? You can also answer that with what you do not want to see.
This is mostly I think about the girls. Some girls come in and they've got heavy makeup on, they've got the high heels, like they're dressed up to look *sexy* and that doesn't help. I think sometimes it's genuinely a distraction, but also that type of clothing is really tight and restrictive. I personally don't really care (what people wear) but that's also me. I want to see someone who's dressed neatly, but for our program you need to be dressed to work. If you come in, as a man, and you have a slim fitting, woven, button-down shirt that has no give and doesn't allow you to move that's a problem. I always ask them to take their shoes off before the audition when we do a warm-up. Then I leave it up to them as to whether they put their shoes back on before they "audition." Some of them do and some of them don't. I guess if I saw someone show up in sweats, that's acceptable attire as a student in the program, but I guess I would think, "this person doesn't really care." But, you know, if somebody comes in with a neat t-shirt and slacks that's totally fine. Short skirts are a problem because I think it makes people... well, you're already nervous enough about exposing your*self*... and I think it's more uncomfortable if their body is exposed too much. I think if your clothes make you self-conscious either because you are uncomfortable in them or because you've dressed to

achieve a certain effect and you are concerned about whether that effect is working on the auditor, I think that's a problem.

Is there anything in particular that you have issues with or that you are aware you react to?
Visible piercings on the face are a problem for me, especially tongue studs. I ask them to take them out. As far as hair goes, it's like in any class, if you're wearing distracting jewelry, bangles or something, and I'm asking you to jump around and they're going to hurt you, that's a problem. Hats - no hats. I try to separate in my mind how much of this is me being a fuddy-duddy - like the pierced septum with the ring that makes people look like livestock, I react really negatively to that. But the [small stud on the side of the nose] I don't mind. Pierced lips I mind, pierced lateral eyebrow I don't mind quite so much. Tongue piercing - no way. Hair - of course I want to be able to see their face - but I can't think if I've ever had other issues with hair.

I recognize how stressful it is to audition - from the inside and the outside. I recognize the desire to 'hide' - I get it. BUT if you want to hide in your life the blunt way to say it is you have no business trying to become an actor. The whole point is that you reveal yourself. All the various schools of actor training in the U.S. and in England say that's what it's about. For me, the thing that excites me the most is when I see someone kind of struggling with that. It can be really moving when you see someone who is scared, but is not being overcome by the nerves; who maybe wants to hide, but overcomes it and then does something good; who is able to process that physically through the body and voice so something comes out. Then they're having a real experience. And that's what I'm constantly talking about with my students: The lines are not your words. There's all this imaginary stuff going on. But the experience that you have as a performer onstage, it is REAL, and there's some real shit going on, and if you engage with that experience, a real thing is happening between you and your [scene] partner and that's exciting. So when you see someone do something like that on whatever level, then you go "AHA! That is it!"

2-8 Joseph Price
The University of Minnesota/Guthrie Theater BFA Actor Training Program
Program Director

What population do you audition?
I recruit undergraduates. However, I spent 11 years at UMKC (University of Missouri Kansas City) where I recruited graduate students, so I have experience in both worlds.
I currently audition for our BFA in Acting.

When the ideal candidate for your program walks into the room, what are you looking for? What do you see?
Students ask that question all the time actually.

It's a difficult question to answer because at the end of the day what we are looking for is "fit." What I mean by that is our program proposes a partnership between the University and a professional company. So we are looking for students that are interested in training while also being surrounded by the profession. We are a classically based program, so heightened text is a big part of what we do. Our program has a conservatory rigor with an academic component.

Since they've signed up and are auditioning, I hope they've done a little bit of research - enough to know that, hey, we do a lot of Shakespeare and we're connected to a major regional theater. I think that's important. I hope one of the reasons they're auditioning is that they understand what we are about! We do get students, I think, who audition just because we are on some list and they heard our program is something they ought to audition for, but it's clear that they have no real understanding of what we're about. So I think finding out what we are about is important.

One of the things we talk about on our website is the fact that we're looking for serious students. So I'm looking for a certain amount of professionalism when they walk through the door. They're serious about this, they're prepared, they are engaged, they are not coming in and there's the feeling of, "well, you know, somebody said I was a good actor so I thought I'd try auditioning." It's important that they're serious because the training is very rigorous. If you're not serious you're not going to make it through the training.

What are your audition requirements?

We ask for three pieces. We ask for a classical piece and a contemporary piece, which are contrasting. And we want one of those to be close to what the student *is*: age-appropriate and energy appropriate, something close to them. And then we ask for a third piece, which we call a stretch piece: what role would you love to play that you'd never be cast as? It's really my favorite part of the audition because we learn so much about them, just even through their choice. The other thing is that sometimes students will make a choice that is a role they *could* play, so that opens up the conversation about why they chose that. That happens all the time. But it's not a wrong choice - it begins a dialogue and then we have a conversation about the choice. So we ask for those three pieces and we want them to be in total about 5 1/2 minutes.

One of the things that happens with students sometimes is that they think they have contrasting material but it's *not* a contrast. It comes across as the same color and the same tone. And often when we get to that third stretch piece we see some completely different aspect of them [the actor].

Regarding the classical piece, do you expect to hear Shakespeare? What are you looking for in a classical piece?

If they don't do Shakespeare we'll ask for it. So if they did their three pieces and they didn't do a Shakespeare, we'd ask for it. So I think it's useful if they do Shakespeare though they don't have to. I think because we're classically based, even if a student doesn't have a lot of experience with Shakespeare, we still want to know that they like language and that somehow they are enthusiastic about language - that language moves them somehow. So we'll get students who are relatively green and have never done Shakespeare, but somehow, through working with the piece we will see that there's something in them that's connected to heightened text, to language. I think it is useful, if they *can* do Shakespeare, that they do.

Do you want it to be in verse?
It's not a rule. Again it's one of those things where, if they did perform their audition and we want to see another piece, we would probably ask for something in verse. But for the three pieces they bring in it's not a rule.

Are there any monologues or types of monologues that you never want to hear again?
I'm not a big fan of monologues about actors or about acting. Some are okay, but I'd rather not hear those kinds of pieces to be honest. Just in terms of overdone, the *Laughing Wild* "tuna fish piece" is so overdone. I say that, and yet I recently saw a kid just kill it a few weeks ago - did a different take that I'd just never seen. But in general that's a piece that I don't like to see.

I think my personal peeve is, well, just stay away from monologues about actors. Other than that…

How many students do you accept into each class?
20.

How many do you see in a season?
In terms of all of the regional auditions and things that we do, which are really screening auditions for us, we see about 1200 to 1300 actors a year. And then those that really get serious and apply at the University comes down to about 400.

What is the ideal audition outfit?
Something that looks professional but allows you to do your work. I don't know if that's too broad…

Is there anything you'd like to add? Anything about auditioning that you think would be particularly helpful for them to know?
Yes. One big thing: when I talk to students or are visiting an art school or high school, one of the things I talk about is "know what play you're auditioning for." In other words, know when you're walking into an audition what our program is about. If you come in and you're way over time, that tells me you didn't really "know the play." We have an expectation. It's on our website. If you come in and you don't do the stretch piece and you just give us three pieces… I think that that's important and often we'll see students who feel like "I'm doing my 10 auditions in Chicago and somebody told me I should audition for your program." But they haven't researched us. And I think that's very important. If you're auditioning for a specific play you'd read the play, you'd know about it, and you'd come in ready to go. You'd be prepared. I guess I feel the same way about auditioning. We're all looking for students that are talented and have potential - that's pretty straightforward. But we're also looking for students who are looking. We are looking across the table and

saying, "do we want to spend four years with this person?" They should be asking the same question.

2-9 John Ray Proctor
Albany State University
Director of Theatre

What degree program do you audition for?
The BA in Speech and Theatre with a Concentration in Theatre.

When an auditionee walks into the room what are you looking for?
Genuine-ness. We are looking for somebody who can listen - if I talk to them, are they listening? Are they genuine in their responses to me? I'm looking to see the *person* without the "performer."
And that's in the greeting, the "hello my name is..."
Is the smile genuine? That's the person I'm looking for.

Then when they start their monologue I want to see them shift to something that says WORK: "what I am doing now is working" - not performing! I'm strangely not looking for "performances" of any sort. I'm looking for a kid who has enough familiarity with the craft to understand that this is *work*, not *performance*.

I'm looking for a level of honesty in their performance.

And then there are some very technical things that I look for: What is their sound like? Where is their voice? Where is their articulation? Where is their centered-ness and rooted-ness? Where is their body and are they relaxed?

When you say "where" do you mean where in their developmental process?
Yes. Where in their developmental process are they? What have they learned in high school? And I think a lot of times one of the things I'm evaluating is how much unlearning will they need to do? I give them direction in the audition to see how much they can accept, take, and go. Are they brave enough to risk trying whatever crazy thing I throw at them?

Where are they in their process? If they are so rooted in their prior training that they can't hear what I'm saying, take it, and run with it…I understand that I will have to un-teach a lot - they will have to unlearn a lot - before this person may really be ready to learn.

How many people do you accept each year into your program?
We accept 12 people into our program each year.

How long is the ideal monologue?
60 to 90 seconds.

Do you ask for two pieces?
I do.

Do you expect to hear Shakespeare?
I do not expect to hear Shakespeare, but I'm delightfully surprised when students say that they're going to give it a shot!

I don't prejudge students. Some of them have *Shakespeare* - some of them are absolutely capable of taking it and making it work.
I'm looking to see: Have they made sense of the language? Do they have any idea what they're talking about? Where are they *in the process of* working with Shakespeare? But I don't require that they do Shakespeare.

I think that we oftentimes throw Shakespeare at students too early. Now, I was at a small school in New Orleans and they were absolutely engaged with Shakespeare. So I don't say that high school students shouldn't do it, but do I require it of them? No.

There's so much work that we do with Shakespeare at our school. We do language training, breathing, physical stuff – all with Shakespeare. So it's one of those things where if they do it I'm in their corner and I'm on their side - "give it your best shot, kid, show me what you got!" But I don't require it.

Are there monologues or types of monologues that you never want to hear again?
One of the things that's interesting about my school is that I teach at an HBCU [Historically Black Colleges and Universities], so there are things that I've seen in auditions that are terrifying! I've seen students who have watched a Tyler Perry movie and then transcribed the dialogue from the movie into a monologue. And they're doing their best impersonation of a character from a Tyler Perry movie. I never want to see that again. But do I judge the student? No.

I am at a small school in rural Georgia and a lot of these kids - it's where they are. Some of them come to me with no training whatsoever and they don't know the difference between theatre and the movies. So I accept where they are - I accept them for where they are in the developmental process. If a kid does a monologue from *Medea Goes To Jail*, I'm not surprised. Now, I will have a conversation with them and say, "maybe that's not your best choice"... But the other thing that I have to think about is that my school is 98% students of color, and I have to be a realist as well. When these kids leave here and go to Atlanta, they *will be auditioning* for Tyler Perry. I can't let my own elitist system stand in the way of the practicalities of them getting a job. So the challenge is how do I get them to do what they're doing better? These are the realities of my world.

Do you have any pet peeves at auditions that you'd like to share?
Oftentimes students are very eager and they stand very, very close to the auditor's table.

One of the things that really gets to me is when they look right into my eyes and expect me to be their scene partner. That's difficult for me. Because I have a different job. My job is to evaluate the work that they are doing, not be their scene partner. When my auditionees insist on engaging with me in that way, that's a pet peeve.

Sometimes they're very quiet - they're nervous, they are shy - and there've been times when I've looked at them and said, "I can't hear you. That was lovely, but I can't hear you. Can you try it again? And your only objective is to get the words *out*."

Sometimes their nerves make them talk very, very fast. These are some of the things that are just technical things, that I find myself giving feedback about in auditions - and then maybe asking them to do it again.

The other *big* thing is fake crying. Lord, I don't want to see that! Some students fake cry throughout their monologues. They are convinced that showing that overwhelming emotion – crying or the yelling kind of "let me show you" anger is what they need to show. And that's not what I'm looking for. So I will give them suggestions to try it another way.

What is the ideal audition outfit?
I want them to wear something that they're comfortable in. I appreciate black slacks, a good button up black shirt, or a black or white T-shirt. I don't want the outfit to distract from my being able to see the work that they're doing.

I have seen young ladies audition in outfits that have plunging necklines, and skirts that are far too short for them... I'm interested in seeing *work*. It's not that I mind that you're a pretty young lady or a handsome young man - these are not problems for me. But it's also not what I'm looking at. I'm not evaluating your marketability for film work. I'm here to teach you the craft of acting. So I want to see that you have come to *work*. Your audition outfit should show respect for yourself, respect for the craft, and respect for me. That's what I would like in your audition outfit.

Is there anything that you want to add?
I think the thing that it took me forever to figure out is that as an actor I spent many, many years *afraid* - afraid of failure, afraid of *so much*. I wasn't doing the work in an audition because I was so terrified about things that didn't matter. It took years of being an actor before I went, "Oh! The auditor just wants to see me *work*! They want to see the honest, rooted work at that I'm doing."

I accept them for whatever they bring into that room, and then these skills are some of the things that we work on in our program. When I talk to my students, that's what I'm teaching them about auditions. When I'm working with my students those are the principles that I'm trying to get across to them: How do we shift from the concept of "performance" to doing good, honest, rooted work? Those are the things we work on.

2-10 Benjamin Reigel
Western Michigan University
Assistant Professor of Theatre - Acting, Shakespeare, Stage Combat

What are you looking for in an audition?
I'll begin this by saying that this is changing for me a little bit. Being fairly new to this side of the table, I would say that when I first started looking for students I was looking, frankly, for certain professional markers that I now realize are silly to be looking for in people coming out of high school. And so I've changed a little bit.

What I am looking for is for them to do, first and foremost, is something that is theatrical. I do want to see a level of theatricality. Are they going to do something big and bold? Is there an inherent sense that they know how to make something happen?

What I'm *not* looking for is just simply someone who's going to get very quiet and have very personal moments - and that's all that ever happens. But I DO want somebody who I can see does bring something of themselves into the room and isn't hiding behind a character. Those two things sound sort of contradictory, but they're not to me. I want something that's bold, I want something that's theatrical, but I also want something that isn't "hiding behind a character."

Is it safe to say you want something bold and theatrical that is based in the truth of the person doing it?
That would be a good way to say it. Yeah - I think it would.

If I'm really answering this *for real*, what I will say is that I am less put off by somebody who is "putting something on" than I think some of my colleagues are. I feel like there is a ton of value in boldness and theatricality, because I think that's hard to teach. And so people who are willing to cloak themselves in a character, even if it's a little crude... I'm finding that I'm interested in that, because that is very hard to get from someone who doesn't naturally have that ability.

And so that is the contradiction in all this. *Yes*, I want to see if somebody has a performer in them. I see students sometimes that say they want to act, and they may manage to find some very small levels of truth, but I don't see any willingness or hunger for actually being theatrical. And I am also hungry for theatricality, which I don't think is a bad thing. I think theatricality sometimes gets confused with falseness, and I don't think those are the same thing at all.

If somebody comes in and does something ridiculous - maybe they do a really big grotesque character that is nothing like them - it doesn't automatically count against them with me, but I'll tell you they're going to have a hard journey with some of the other people in the room. So it's important that they also be able to drop it. And simplify.

If somebody comes in and does something that is way outside of their experience - suppose they picked the wrong piece and they're doing an old character man - I don't necessarily shut off to them just because they're doing something they shouldn't be doing if they're being theatrical and interesting about it. But that's going to make it absolutely necessary that the other piece that they do is simple. Or if we work with them, they'd better be able to drop into simplicity.

What do you want to see in the human being, the actor, when they come in?
I was taught at a young age that you should come in and have confidence and all those things. It's true - those things can help. But just because somebody comes in and they are nervous, that is not a strike against them. Sociopaths are really good at making first impressions right? So they don't need to come in and be all put together.

I'm looking for somebody who is friendly, who looks me in the eye even if they're nervous doing it, somebody who does not appear to be an emotional wreck. Sometimes people walk in and you can see that they're just hanging on by a thread. That worries me a little bit. It worries me. Because I wonder, "how much maintenance am going to have to do?" So I want somebody who is healthy. Okay... If you're nervous, be nervous. It's okay! If you're calm, you're calm! But I want to see what the pressure is doing for them... *to* them. Are they somebody who, when the pressure's getting to them, they fill it up with a ton of bravado and come across as cocky? That's not what I'm looking for. Are they somebody who decides they are going to make it funny that they're nervous and they're just going to be a spaz? That's not really ideal either.

I want somebody who I believe - underneath whatever nerves are going on - is a good, sane listener – they are present. Can they listen despite all of the noise going on in their head?

I appreciate the observation that socio-paths are capable of looking put together - that they're the best at it!
Yes! And they are very good at it, but that doesn't mean that I want to teach them for four years.

How long is the ideal monologue?
For me? 45 seconds. 35 ain't bad either.
The caveat is that it [the monologue] can go longer if it's full of so many changes that I never get comfortable watching it - that I never decide what it is. As soon as I know what it [the action of the monologue] is, it needs to change or be over.

Are there any monologues or types of monologues that you simply never want to see again?
Well yes. I used to have actual monologues I didn't want to see anymore. I can still say I don't want to see anything from *Promedy* – the monologues are terrible for auditions – I'm sorry if the playwright is reading this. I just want monologues that are *good*. I want people to pick things that are well written. And I'm open-minded, but conventional wisdom is that you should pick something from a play.

As for monologue books, NO! The monologues in monologue books are story monologues. I want monologues in which someone is trying to change something about somebody else. So rather than the monologue where you're talking to your psychiatrist or the audience or your best friend about the terrible thing that happened in the past, I want the monologue where you're experiencing the terrible thing and trying to stop it from happening. So instead of, "Oh and then I found him lying in a pool of blood..." which is telling me about something that happened, I want the monologue which is you talking the person out of killing themselves or something like that. Which is, "Hey, you! Put the knife down!" I want them *doing* something.

There are times when someone comes in and does a monologue and you know that they picked it because they simply love the monologue itself. They love the point that it makes, or, worst of all, it has a great punch line and they just really want to say the punch line. But it doesn't tell me anything about them as a person. If your monologue is a comic monologue but the joke is at the very end of the monologue that's not good. Because it means that I have to wait, and I'm not getting any information about *you* while I wait. I love the play *The Nerd*. I love the play! But there's a monologue people do from *The Nerd*, which is him telling the story about being on a plane and it ends with a very funny punch line about people urinating on the plane. But it's a minute and a half monologue to *get to that punch line* - and you really can't trim it. So I think it's a terrible monologue to pick for an audition. Great in the play, but a terrible monologue for an audition.

I don't like it when it's all self-indulgent, which means it's about you just experiencing something. If I ask you "who are you talking to?" and you don't have a good answer, or if the answer is "it doesn't matter," don't do that monologue. The person you're talking to should matter!

Don't do the tuna fish monologue from *Laughing Wild*.

What is the ideal addition outfit? What do you want to see or not want to see?
I'll talk about the men first. Men have it so much easier. Men have fewer choices, which makes it easier. For men, don't look grubby, but don't look like you're applying for a loan. Whatever looks good on your body - show yourself off right.
Are you dumpy? And is that the kind of role you want to play? Then that's fine. If you want to look like the dude who sits around and plays World of Warcraft, that's fine if that's your type. But have some idea of what your type is. And I'm talking a broad range. Don't get narrow about "type".

Are you a very studious person? Are those roles you are going to play? Then dress up a little more.

Just don't look grubby. Look like you care. It doesn't have to be dress-up. I think jeans are fine. Personally, I wear jeans when I audition and a nice button-down shirt, untucked, most of the time. Unless I'm auditioning for something very specific, that kind of outfit suits me - it fits my sort of blue-collar-ness, without looking like I just got done working. It's kind of middle-of-the-road.

Choose based on your body. For example, I personally rarely wear my shirt tucked in because I'm short, and if I tuck my shirt in it cuts me in half and it makes me look shorter. I personally wouldn't wear a sport coat. But that's just me because of the pieces I'm doing. I'm not doing the types of pieces that would require a sport coat. It's not my type.

With men I find it pretty simple - I don't think men tend to distract as much with their clothing.

For *everybody*, don't wear something that is ridiculously distracting. Don't wear a T-shirt if it's got writing on it. Generally speaking, probably don't wear a T-shirt, but definitely don't wear a T-shirt that has writing on it. Don't wear tons of bracelets and necklaces, and chains, and bandanas, and the wallet with the chain going to it, or boots that make a ton of noise when you walk. Just simple things like that. Things that should be common sense, but aren't so much. Because we live in a society that really permits people to dress however they want.

And that's okay, but just be aware of the message you are sending.

I think for women it's way harder. Women have more options. And I'm going to speak as a man watching women's auditions. Don't dress up too much - don't dress like you're going to a cocktail party. If you don't wear heels regularly, don't wear heels in an audition. Don't wear distracting shoes. If my eye goes right to your shoes, that's not good. I think that happens probably 40% of the time. Sometimes it's because they're really nice expensive shoes that don't match the outfit, or it's that they match but you look like you're dressed for the wrong occasion.

One of the things that we see that is a problem is women who come in wearing perfectly nice clothes, but then they wear UGG boots. It's just a bad look.

I can't tell you how many times lovely women have come in dressed like they just came out of the bunker from *The Unbreakable Kimmy Schmidt*. It's as if they're doing everything they can to hide the fact that they're attractive. And I think the same is sometimes true for men, but less often.

If you have an amazing body you can let us know that without looking like you're trying to sell an audition based on that alone. There are men who are in great shape, but you don't need to come in wearing a speedo for me to know that. And the same thing goes for women. For some women, their body is going to be a major selling point for the type of parts they're going to play, but that doesn't mean that they have to wear a skirt that's super short and a low-cut blouse, just to sell that. We can see what's happening.

And don't hide behind your hair. I need to see your face, whether you like your face or not, I need to see your face – and that goes for men and women both. Men shouldn't have beards. That's important. With this hipster movement - I mean, I don't mean to sound like an old man talking about "these young hipsters" [old man voice], but with this hipster thing beards are now in style for men. And men, for a training program audition you should be clean-shaven. And in your headshot you should be clean-shaven. We need to see your face. We have no idea what you look like under facial hair. Show me your face!

I will point out to the reader that Ben is quite young, and is not an old fogie.
He just sounds like a 90-year-old man!

Is there anything you want to add? Is there anything you think is important for people auditioning to know?
We really do want them to do well. Seriously. We may look grumpy when you look at us. Some of us have faces that look really un-amused. But we might be having a great time - you don't know. We really do want you to do well.

And also, the time is *yours*! I will illustrate this from my experience, because I have much more experience as an auditionee than as an auditor: I used to sometimes know walking out of the room that I was apologizing for doing my audition while I was doing it. And it's a terrible feeling. And now that I'm sitting on the auditor side of the table, it's made me a better auditionee. Because I truly now "get" that they want me to succeed in a way that I didn't get it before. *You don't need to apologize!* You're not wasting anybody's time. Go in there and take the time (make sure your pieces are the right length, follow the rules) but take the time you are allotted. I mean *take the time that is yours. Own* the time that is yours. You are better off giving a kick ass audition where they call time on you than you are rushing through an audition. We don't forget that the person was amazing just because the timer may have stopped them. If the two minutes I saw was great I'm not gonna forget that.

Make sure that your two pieces are clearly delineated from each other. I can't tell you how many times I can't tell that a person has switched pieces because their eyes didn't move, and they sound the same.

And another thing: if you're doing more than one piece, make sure that you're selling something different in each piece. And are you doing different things with the two pieces? People can get very thrown off because they know the shows their pieces come from and the shows may seem very different to them. But out of context, the two pieces may be selling the same thing about you. In a tragic piece you may be selling that you are anxious and speaking from the heart and really nervous, and in the second piece you may be anxious and nervous and speaking from the heart but it's from a comedy. It's still the same thing. So sell me something different. Have the courage to sell me something different! That's what I want to see.

2-11 Phil Timberlake
The Theatre School at DePaul University
Associate Professor of Voice and Speech

Phil Timberlake auditions and recruits for both the BFA Acting and MFA Acting programs. Information specifically for MFA candidates appears with the MFA interviews in Part 4.

When an ideal candidate for either of your programs walks into the room, what are you looking for?
I'm looking for someone who is open and available and excited to be in the room and to do some work with us - someone who seems more or less confident in an admittedly awkward situation. (Laughs)

What are your general audition guidelines?
The BFA students prepare one contemporary monologue, 45 seconds to 2 minutes in length. We also teach a group class for 45 minutes. We do some voice work and movement work and acting work - just to see them work and to get to know them a little bit. (And they get to know us, too!) That's about a 90-minute process. And then we have a same-day call back. The callback (with a different group of faculty) includes performing the monologue again, some cold reading, and open scene work.

How long is the ideal monologue?
Personally speaking? I would say a minute and a half. But I know almost everything I need to know in 20 seconds. That's the truth. I suppose to give time for a piece to have a beginning, a middle, and an end, and giving people a chance to (maybe in the midst of their nervousness) lose focus for a moment and regain it requires more than 20 seconds. I would say that 90 seconds gives you a chance to deal with all of that. But I ultimately know most of what I need to know in 20 or 30 seconds. So going beyond the time requirements that are listed, going beyond two minutes, personally begins to feel rude. I start to question their generosity of spirit. We've had Shakespeare monologues go for 3 1/2 or 4 minutes. And at that point I just start to think, "This is about you, not about me."

Are there any monologues or types of monologues that you simply never want to hear again?
You know I hesitate to name any, primarily because they change over time. There are monologues that we used to

hear all the time that we hardly ever hear anymore. And there are new ones coming up that leave us thinking, "yeah, now we are going to hear the character Ken from *Red* by John Logan for the next three years." These things come up. But the reason I hesitate to say "don't do that monologue again" is because I want people to come in with a monologue that they have a personal connection to – in terms of the given circumstances, in terms of the "other" that they're talking to. If that is the case, then they are going to reveal more about themselves and that will tell me more about my desire to work with them for three or four years.

Then the other thing, and this is specifically for the BFA candidates, because I can't recall an MFA candidate who's ever done this... Bring in a monologue from an actual play. You can pretty much smell monologues that were written just to be monologues a mile away. And I have never seen one in which the world the character inhabits is big enough. So when somebody says, "I'll be doing The Breakup by James Smith", the monologue is *all* about a breakup. It's simply never rich enough; it's *never* rich enough. So I would say do a monologue from a play. And do something that you're connected to, and in which you're passionate about the character, and the circumstances are there, and the connection enlivens your imagination and desire to speak these words, now, for this purpose. And if that's the case then I'll listen to you. And also because we take time to work with the students, the monologue isn't the only thing we look at. It's just one piece of the puzzle.

What is the ideal audition outfit? What sorts of things do you not want to see?

The extremes are the things to avoid - things that are impossible to move in, things that are excessively revealing of the body, and also things that are incredibly casual. Those extremes I think are to be avoided. Now, with the BFA students – they're 18-year-olds, so I have a lot of grace. I'm not going to discount people based on what they wear because oftentimes they don't know. (Which is why you're writing the book, right?) But I would say wear something - especially for the monologue portion of it - something where you look nice. You look *nice* in this. It doesn't have to be a tie, it doesn't have to be a suit, and it doesn't have to be a dress. And you should be able to move - in other words you can be on your feet acting in it. So high heels or anything that limits your ability to do that is a problem. And specifically for our program we suggest that for the second half, for the class period, that they also have clothes that they can change into that they can just move in. Sweatpants, yoga pants, whatever - stuff where they can get down on the floor and roll around. That's very specific to our procedures.

But yes, things where you feel like you look nice, where you are "presentable" as my grandmother would say, and you're not going to be limited.

Regarding auditionees changing clothes for the movement portion of the audition: Do you or do people on your team keep track of people based on what they are wearing?
We take photos of them, so when they change we are able to keep track of them. We also see them in groups of 10-15, so it's not a huge cattle call. However, I think what you might be getting at is, "would it be a good idea to wear a red shirt for your audition and then a red shirt for the class portion?" and yes, I think that would be a great idea.

But we know that since we've asked them to change, the onus is on us to keep track of who they are. But is it a bad idea if they wear a blue button-down shirt for the monologue to also wear blue T-shirt for the movement portion? No, that's not a bad idea at all.

Is there anything you want to add?
This is what I would say, I would say for the BFA's especially, don't feel like you have to "capital P" Perform for us. What we are looking for is somebody who we want to work with; somebody that we want to train for the next four years. And the thing is, that we want you to come in and play. One of the questions we ask a lot is, "Are they *Game*?" Because this is an intense conservatory. You have to play, and play well with others. And acting is not about "performing." We start with the work on the self. For example: if we ask you to just walk through the space, that's actually what we mean. Not "perform" walking through the space. And there have been BFA actors who, even though I give the prompt, don't seem to be able to let go of the "I'm performing"

mentality…. There are people I have not passed on to the callback process because I don't know if they understand what that means.

It's also not about performing "the ideal monologue." Really we are looking for something you're passionate about, in which you have some understanding of the given circumstances. Connecting to an imaginary partner is hard, hard work. Find ways to practice that with a real partner, with a real person, in various ways in various rooms so that you really have a sense of connecting to this imaginary partner, which is so difficult. It's not that you're not going to Nail it (with a capital N.) You will not Nail your audition. It is not possible to Nail an audition. Not for our program. It's not going to happen. What we are going to see is how you work over the 90 minutes we have with you. If that shows us something where we think, "hey this might be a fit," then you've got another 90 minutes at the callback. It's about that process of "how do you work?" And do we feel like you would fit into the way we work in this little community.

2-12 David Williams
University of Miami
Professor of Theater
Director of Graduate Studies

Degrees offered: BFA in Acting, BFA in Musical Theater
This interview will focus on the auditions for the BFA in Acting.

How many students do you accept each year into the program?
20. (This is a total for the Conservatory. Both Acting and Musical Theatre.)

How many do you see each year?
350 to 500.

Let's talk about an ideal candidate for your acting program. When they walk into the room what is it that you see, or feel, or experience?
We really look for people that we like immediately. Immediate personality - we want to know that this is someone that we want to live with for four years. We are a small program, and so we need to make sure that their personality jives with ours. Of course, talent. And the ability to be human in the room. Not just coming at us like a shotgun like some kids are trained to do.

We want to see how they react to whatever dumb things we ask them to do - on purpose sometimes, just to see what they do with it.

Also, what is it that they want from a theatre education? We expect them to really answer the question, not just give us a rote answer. We are looking for actually nice people with brains and talent. Just talent alone won't do it. They've got to be good people too.

What do you ask for in auditions?
What is listed right now is two contrasting monologues, preferably one with heightened language but not necessarily Shakespeare. We also ask them to sing something, even if they are auditioning for just straight acting. All of our acting majors have been in musicals. So we see if they are "game" to do that. You know, it's just another chance to see what they're willing to do.

What if they absolutely can't sing?
I think we have to figure out if that's actually the truth. An actor needs a good ear - period. So I'm not sure that I would actually believe that.

How long do you want the monologues to be?
Short and full of wonderment - so not very long. Because what I really like is a short audition and then more time to work on the audition material with them. I want to see what they're willing to do. I think all of us can tell within three words whether we like the kid or not. So I'd like to use as much of the remaining time as possible to work with them. I find that the time gets tighter and tighter as we get more and more people wanting to audition.

How long a monologue do you need to see?
It actually depends on the kid. Some of them need a little extra time to warm into it and I'm fine with that. If they've

been trained well, the shorter the better. If they've been trained well they can usually get right to the nitty-gritty. For me it really isn't about the audition material, it's about the audition itself.

Are there any monologues or types of monologues that you simply never want to hear again?
I suppose there are. But I think if somebody is really good at something I will want to watch.

I think this is one of the places where some of the information out there can be less useful. I think there are people charging kids - saying they can guarantee the right material, saying they know the "secrets of auditioning" - and that sort of thing. So much of it is so wrong - just misguided and basically moneygrubbing. Without getting into a war with those people that are doing that, I would rather just say that whatever the piece is, I would like it to be as age-appropriate as possible. I personally don't particularly like monologues that are attacks on professors. It's like with the musical theatre stuff - there are certain songs that I don't particularly want to hear, but it wouldn't be the material itself that keeps them from getting into our school. While they are here we teach them to have good taste in material and to learn good audition technique. But age appropriateness is nice. I don't particularly like to hear a lot of strong language coming from the mouths of 17-year-olds. I just find it odd. None of us are prudes, but I'd rather have joyous material.

Every once in a while I'll torture myself by reading some of these websites that are dedicated to "how to get into schools." And I just wind up screaming at the screen, because some of the observations are just so full of baloney. You know, the idea that parents can ever know for sure why their kids did or didn't get into school... it's just ridiculous! You know there's so much involved that I can't control. There are certain aspects of the admissions process that the university has to do before I can even have a say. You know, they [admissions] are willing to let me fight for a kid but if the kid can't get into the university academically, then no matter what their talent is, I can't accept them. And I think that's an important thing that they really need to know when they're going to programs that are housed in real universities: there is a fundamental difference between my program and a program that may be housed in a conservatory. We have an academic portion that they really, really have to pay attention to. And that is part of our contract with the parent: they are going to get a good education also.

What is the ideal audition outfit? Do you have observations about things that do or do not work?
What an interesting question. I am not one who usually criticizes people for what they're wearing. My colleagues always have shoe issues for some reason.

Sensible, ready to work clothes - you know, not glamorous outfits. Going for the glamour kind of makes me crazy.

I guess I'm biased, but I think someone that looks like they're ready to go to work is what I prefer to see: simple, not obtrusive, something that looks like they're ready to get down to work. But frankly, if they come in dressed brilliantly I like it (laughs). So I guess I'm not sure exactly where I fall on this. I do have to say that extremely high-heeled shoes seem to piss everybody off. I don't particularly care, but my colleagues always, always have issues if their heels are high.

Is there anything you would like to add?
Yes. Probably a lot.

Parents are an interesting conundrum when it comes to auditions. The ones that hover around the audition door and make themselves known almost better than their students - I think their behavior needs to be a little less intrusive. It doesn't help. It often... It hurts. I think an over-active stage parent can actually cause me not to want to have their kid in my program. I don't know how to gently say that, but occasionally we run into parents in the audition process who leave us wondering if we want to deal with four years of that type of overactive stage parenting. It does paint a picture that is not positive. And we see it in auditions all the time.

A couple of years into their training, I often ask kids where their parents were when they auditioned - whether they came with them - and it turns out that many, many of the kids I ended up accepting actually banned their parents from the audition. Other than just carting them to the audition itself.

I think there has to be a way of putting out there the idea that parents need to let their kids prepare their auditions completely on their own. The parents really can't do the acting for them, and they really can't improve their auditions.

I will reference your interview in Part 5, which is written for parents and supportive others. Along with helping them not be freaked out about the fact that their kid wants to get a degree in theatre, I would like them to understand how important it is that they not be a "helicopter" parent, and absolutely not a "snowplow" parent - that it doesn't help the auditionee at all. Sometimes we know the parents better than we know their kids.
Yes! Oh, absolutely.

There is definitely a time in the process when the parents can ask any question they want, but it's not at the audition. Pick up the phone and call me while I'm not auditioning kids, and I'll spend as much time as necessary. I won't discuss the kid's talent, under any circumstances, but we can talk about the program and that sort of stuff. There is definitely a time and place for parental questions, but the audition is for the kid, and the kid only. It's important that it not be made about the parent, because that will hurt. It actually hurts.

Is there anything else?
It's really important to me that the kids find the material on their own.

I agree. I do coach, but I give them guidelines on material, and then they have to go find their own material. I also feel that's very important.
Yes!

Oh! I remembered something I really want to say:
There is no advantage in doing the Unified auditions over an on campus audition, or vice versa. They each have their own value. I am asked this all the time - because people hear that it's better to come to campus because their chances of getting in are better. That is absolutely not true! The advantage of going to the campus auditions is that you get to see the school, versus going to New York, Chicago, or LA. The advantage of going to the New York, Chicago, or LA auditions is that you are in this place that is all about auditioning. All these other people also there to audition creates an energy. And that energy can help carry you through the audition. I think that's an important point. There are advantages both ways!

What a nice way to put that! I appreciate that!

One of the things that I'm most proud of at our university is that I am told that our auditions are a great thing, that we treat the auditionees well. And that is something I am very, very proud of.

And whenever you want to hit the music theatre trail on this, I'm there for you.

That is a whole other type of beast, but I am realizing that it will probably need to be done.
I think more of the "crazy" audition behavior comes from the musical theatre portion of it. There's a lot of stuff that needs clarification. And of course, there are more of those [musical theatre] auditions out there.

You know, I would love to see an uptick in the musical theatre students auditioning for straight acting programs. I don't know whether it's that people just see dollar signs, or really just love the joy of musical theatre, but I'd really like to see people be better *actors*. I'd like to see that for sure. Without the acting chops, I'm just not interested!

Part 3

Auditioning For Graduate Training Programs

3-1 Preparing your audition

The mechanics of auditioning presented in Part 1 apply to graduate training programs as well as undergraduate training programs. The expectations are higher at the graduate level, however, as there are fewer graduate training programs and each program accepts fewer students. For that reason, everything in Part 1 must be carefully attended to and executed to the best of your ability.

This section offers additional considerations that apply to auditions at the graduate training level.

What are auditors looking for at the graduate level?
Auditors in graduate training auditions are looking for more specific qualities than those auditioning students for undergraduate training. You will notice as you read the interviews in Part 4 that the answers are often very specific. This *does not* mean that you should try to "be what they want". You be yourself.

Auditors are looking for talent and potential, but they are also assessing your skill level. They need to see where you are in your training. They need to assess your current level of expertise so they can determine whether what you offer and what their program offers is a good fit.

Get good coaching
If you are auditioning for graduate training programs, you need to be on your game. If you are ready for a graduate program, a certain level of mastery is expected. For this reason, it is important to work with a coach if at all

Elizabeth Terrel

possible. A good coach offers a practiced eye and an external viewpoint.

Good coaching does not aim to shape you into something you are not or to make you "perfect." If anyone ever tells you they will give you the "perfect monologue" or that they can "guarantee" placement in a program, run - don't walk – away!

Know who you are and how you will likely be cast
This is where "type" comes in. Know who you are and how you are seen and make your audition choices accordingly. I'm not suggesting the idea of "type" as a limitation, but as an honest assessment of how you will most likely be cast.

For example, when I auditioned for graduate school I was in my 30's and was a 5'6" woman with dark hair, strong arched eyebrows, and a strong but shapely body. I was not overweight, but I was also not waif-like. I had muscular articulation skills and a powerful speaking voice. If I had auditioned with a Juliet monologue it would have sent a strong message that I did not know who I was or how I would likely be cast. That would have been a huge red flag. Graduate training programs are looking for actors who are ready for professional training. Knowing who you are and how you will be cast is one of the signs of a professional.

Again, a coach can be helpful here. It is hard to be objective about ourselves. And it's incredibly important that you have an understanding of who you are and how you will most likely be cast. It is a strong, positive cue to the auditors when you choose your pieces wisely and dress appropriately. It lets them easily see that YOU know who you are.

3-2 Your classical monologue

Do a classical monologue

At this level a classical monologue is expected. The auditors need to assess how you handle heightened language and heightened thought.

Verse? Prose? Shakespeare?

For years I have been asking graduate school auditors about classical piece selection. Some directly state that they expect to hear Shakespeare and they expect to hear verse, as verse requires a skill level that prose does not. Most auditors state that the classical piece does not *have* to be Shakespeare, but as we talk, it becomes apparent that if given a choice, they'd really rather hear Shakespeare.

Therefore, I would recommend that when selecting a classical piece it is safest to select a Shakespeare monologue that is in verse. This way you have met the requirement of the most particular auditors and those less particular will be fine with your choice. And obviously your selection needs to be appropriate in age and energy to you – in other words, a role in which you would likely be cast.

What about the Greeks? Moliere?

I personally would not recommend one of the Greeks as a classical piece. You simply can't depend on the translations – some are more sophisticated than others and it can be hard to find one that lets the auditors assess your skill level well. And while the Greeks often encompass the grand size and scope of Shakespeare, they do not generally demand the same specific language skills or match the complexity of thought. I am obviously generalizing here, as there no doubt are exceptions. The thing is that auditors are used to seeing people do less sophisticated translations of Greek monologues, so even if you choose a great one they are going to have to listen closely to the piece itself to see if the monologue is giving you the opportunity to show off your skills. It's really better if all their observational energy is focused on you rather than on the quality of the monologue itself.

Some auditors enjoy Moliere as a classical selection, or some of Shakespeare's contemporaries. If you *really* don't want to do Shakespeare, there *are* good alternatives. What you seek is complex thought, verse construction (rhyming you have to make sound natural), and sophisticated argument.

It is no doubt clear that I recommend you just do Shakespeare. The level of complexity lets the auditors see what they are looking for, the pieces are of good quality, and the energy spent assessing other material could be invested in preparing your audition.

What you must do as you prepare
For your Shakespeare piece there are things that are vital for graduate training auditions:
1) Be word perfect. Most auditors know most of these monologues. Be word perfect. Period.
2) Make sure all pronunciations are right and that you know the meanings of all the words in the monologue within the context of the play. There

are many resources available to do this. Use a Lexicon and a pronouncing dictionary specific to Shakespeare.

3) Pronounce all names correctly – do not assume that pronunciations that may seem obvious to you are correct.

Monologues to avoid

There are some pieces that schools and URTA (more information to come) specifically ask you *not* to do, and some that auditors just don't want to see because they are overdone. The ones that are most consistently on this list are Launce from *The Two Gentlemen of Verona* and Phoebe from *As You Like It*.

Additionally, if you do Hamlet, you'd better bring your "A game." And I personally would not recommend "To be or not to be..." – if you must do Hamlet, I would suggest selecting one of his other monologues.

Also know that crazy is hard – even if you do it well, it is harder for auditors to see who you are through the piece. Lady M and Ophelia both have monologues they speak *before* they lose their minds. I personally think it's best to do one of their "sane" monologues.

3-3 Making good clothing choices

At this level you are expected to know how to market yourself – which is what monologue selection and clothing choices are about.

Pay attention to the clothing guidelines in Part 1. It is not the job of the auditors to see past poor clothing choices, and sometimes the choices people make are so poor that they *just can't see the person.*

While watching graduate school auditions I have made the following notes:
"Is her body very unusually proportioned or is it that over shirt?"
"I think she has great legs but can't tell with those baggy boots"
"Is she pregnant or is it the blouse?"
"I CANNOT EVEN SEE HIS FACE! GET YOUR HAIR OUT OF YOUR FACE!!!"
"All those scarves! Is she in there?"
"Sneakers with a suit...ugh"

It is incredibly frustrating to be searching for fantastic actors but have people who *might* be fantastic wearing things that are so distracting we cannot even tell what they actually look like! At the graduate level the competition is tough. Make your clothing, accessory, and hair choices wisely so the auditors can see what they need to see: YOU at your auditioning actor best.

It may be a good idea to hire a professional image consultant. As an actor, your looks and personal presentation will matter for the rest of your career, so professional guidance is a wise investment. Be sure you work with someone who understands the acting profession. You do not need to look like you are dressing for a job interview; you need to look like you are dressing for an audition.

Common mistakes at the graduate level:
Wrong age bracket Choose type and age appropriate clothing. If you are an adult, there are clothing choices you need to avoid: baby-doll dresses of any kind, leggings masquerading as pants, shoes that make you totter around because they are too high, gym shoes, sandals and flip-flops, sweats, and anything that is for the "20 and under" crowd.
Dressing too formally This is not a wedding. If you wear a suit, you are probably overdressed. If you insist on a suit you must take the jacket off so they can see your shape and how you move and you must wear dress shoes – no sneakers with anything dressy. (Just no sneakers at all please.)
Casual Friday This *might* be a good look for you if you are the guy who gets the "I came to fix the copier" roles. But generally Casual Friday clothes (khakis and a polo shirt) are kind of a traditional, boring costume that may both restrict your movement and hide your actual personality.
"I just rolled out of bed looking like this" This is too casual. Your clothes should be clean, relatively wrinkle free, in good shape, match, and be attractive.
Too revealing, too sexy If you are a beautiful, shapely woman (or man, but this is more common for women) who will get work because of your beauty, the auditors

can see that. They will recognize your beauty and your figure as long as you don't wear *layers* of clothing. Wearing low-cut or super short or revealing clothing just makes everyone uncomfortable.

Review the above guidelines about clothing and the suggestions in Part 1 and take them seriously. If you're auditioning for graduate training, there is an assumption that you are an adult. I repeat - if you have a hard time figuring out what to wear, this is the time to invest in the services of an image consultant.

You also do not need lots of audition outfits. You really only need one good outfit. You may get tired of it, but the auditors won't – they only see you in it once, maybe twice. So one good audition outfit is something you invest in and wear over and over. You do not need to spend a lot of money on this audition outfit, but you do need to make a wise choice.

Make good clothing choices. Clothing can be a huge distraction if it is wrong.

Do not let poor clothing choices keep the auditors from seeing your potential, your skill, your self-awareness, and your talent.

3-4 Preparing your body

Achieve and maintain a healthy level of fitness
Graduate school auditors are looking for actors who will be able to work in the industry. They are looking for actors who have the strength and stamina to succeed in the often very physical world of theatre. They are also assessing whether auditionees will do well with the rigors of graduate school training. This does not mean you must be bikini-ready or look like a superhero. Fit bodies come in a wide variety of shapes and sizes. Fit bodies are, however, as strong and flexible as body type allows.

If you are preparing for graduate training auditions and are not in your best shape and don't have much time, don't sweat it – by all means you should pursue your dream! But if you have time to get in better shape, do it.

3-5 Why graduate training and why now?

A graduate program is generally three years of concentrated study with a small group of people. It is intense. Different programs are intense in different ways, but make no mistake – you will live and breathe acting for the duration of your time in graduate training.

You *will* be asked "Why graduate training and why now?"
Graduate training is a big commitment. Why do you want to go? And *why now?*

Some undergraduate students preparing for graduation erroneously think of graduate training as a natural "next step." It is not. Most programs would, frankly, prefer a candidate with experience in their craft and a bit more life experience. Most take a select few candidates right out of undergraduate training, but they don't accept many of them. Graduate school is rigorous. It is not something to do because you don't know what else to do. Think long and hard about whether it is the right choice for you at this time.

Be prepared to answer the question "Why graduate training and why now?" truthfully.

3-6 Statement of Purpose

Most graduate schools will ask you for a Statement of Purpose, or something to that effect. Ideally, I would recommend that you prepare this before you even begin the graduate school audition process. It will help you answer the *why go and why now?* question. It also may help you determine what type of program is right for you.

Ideally, your Statement of Purpose is a one-page paper that tells the reader who you are as a person and an artist and what you stand for. Step by step instructions are in Part 1.

As a graduate training auditionee, you may have been out of school for a while, so this may sound daunting. Your Statement of Purpose needs to be well written and free of typographical errors. You will need a good proofreader. If you know people with fantastic writing skills who can proofread for you, ask for their help. You may also want to contact the writing center at a college near you. Help with projects like this is available at many community colleges.

The best advice I can give you about writing your Statement of Purpose is:
1) Start by writing a much longer document than is required. Begin by writing everything you can think of that relates to you as an artist and to your artistic purpose. Since you are writing a one-page paper, start by writing at least three or four pages.
2) Review what you've written (by yourself or with help from someone who understands the purpose

of the document) and take out all the general statements that anyone else could make, i.e.: "I want to make a difference"; "I want to help people"; "Art can change the world".

3) Provide specific answers. There is certainly nothing wrong with the above sentiments – many of us share these sentiments. But this is your *personal* statement of purpose, so it needs to be specific. If you want to do your art to change the world, tell your reader *why*. What do you want to change? Why? How?

If writing is not your strong suit
You may want to start by recording yourself – just start talking about the subject. Or ideally have a friend interview you. Then listen to the recording and write down what you said.

Be brave
Be brave. Share your heart. Tell your readers why you want more training. Be honest. If they make you an offer and you accept it, you will spend a lot of time with them and they will know you well. Give them the truth about who you are so they will know if you are right for their program and if their program is right for you. You don't want to get into just *any* program – you want to get into the program that is *right for you*.

3-7 Your Headshot, your Resume, and asking for Letters of Recommendation

Headshots

These must be professional if you are auditioning for graduate training. This is professional level training and you must be a professional in the process and look like one.

You probably already have professional headshots if you've been working professionally. If you don't, follow the guidelines in Part 1. How much this will cost depends on where you are in the country. What matters is that you have a professional quality headshot with excellent lighting that *looks like you*.

Your resume

Follow the guidelines in Part 1. If you are auditioning for graduate training programs you likely have a professional resume at this point.

Depending on how long you've been in the professional market, you may still have undergraduate productions on your resume. That is okay.

Do list your undergraduate institution under "Training" or "Education" and list your undergraduate instructors with their areas of expertise. Many of us know one another.

Letters of recommendation

At this level, you will be asked at some point for letters of recommendation. These letters will be submitted without you seeing them – you will likely be asked to "waive the right to review" the letters. This means you should select your references carefully.

1) Select individuals who will give you excellent references.
2) Contact individuals you would like to list as references *in advance* and ask them if they are willing to serve as a reference for you. If they encourage you to use someone else, do it. Perhaps they are just busy, but it may be their way of saying they cannot give you as positive a reference as you might like.
3) At least one of your letters of reference should be from someone with whom you have trained so they can speak to their experience of you as a student.
4) Select individuals who write well.

3-8 The URTA auditions

What is URTA?

URTA stands for University Resident Theatre Association
www.urta.com
URTA is a consortium of graduate schools (MFA degree granting) and professional theatre training programs and partnered professional theatre companies. Visit the website for more information about the organization.

The URTA auditions are held in major markets in the U.S. where member schools gather and hold auditions. This gives you the opportunity, for a fee, to audition for many programs at once.

The URTA audition requirements are posted on the website each year. Auditionees perform their auditions in a large room in which auditors from multiple schools have gathered.

The process is spelled out on the URTA website and in registration materials each year. But here are some general things to know:
♦ Registration is in the fall - usually the deadline is in November, but check early in the fall and don't miss the deadline for registration.
♦ Not all programs audition candidates at all locations, so if there's a school you particularly want to audition for, check with them and make sure they'll be there.
♦ Not all programs accept students every year. Some programs take in new students only every two or three years.

♦ Plan to stay an extra day in case you get many callbacks.

♦ Make sure you have access to the internet onsite so you can research schools that call you back.

♦ Do not pre-judge. You may think you know absolutely which program you want to go to - and you may be wrong. Keep an open mind.

♦ Just because a school makes you an offer doesn't mean you have to accept it.

♦ Don't stand up a school at call-backs. It's rude. It's also a small world. If you absolutely can't consider attending a school that called you back, do them the courtesy of letting them know so they are not sitting and waiting for you. Be considerate.

♦ A thank you note or email following a callback is appreciated.

♦ If you get many callbacks, you may be very, very busy with no breaks. Take water and something to snack on along with the other items in your audition bag.

Non-URTA auditions

Programs that are not URTA programs often hold auditions by appointment or on a walk-in basis in the same hotels as the URTA auditions, so you can audition for URTA programs and non-URTA programs all in one general location. The fee for the URTA auditions does not cover the fees for auditioning for non-URTA programs.

Satellite auditions

Some non-URTA programs participate in Satellite auditions in which you can audition for participating programs en masse. Not all programs participate. Be sure you schedule auditions with programs that interest you if they do not participate in the Satellite auditions.

Callbacks
If a training program is interested in you, they will ask for a callback. Callbacks are usually held in a hotel room, so don't be surprised by that – it is normal.

At callbacks you may work pieces, just sit and talk, or do any variety of things. It is wise to wear clothing in which you can move and work.

You do not need to wear the same outfit to callbacks as you did to auditions, but it's okay if you do. They are assessing you and your talent and will not frown on your wearing the same clothing as long as it allows you to move freely, is flattering, and is still clean and fresh.

Personal opinion This is by no means a rule, but I think it's a good idea to wear the same basic colors to callbacks as you do to the monologue audition. Some auditors don't notice what color you're wearing at all, but some of us do. For those of us who do, staying in the same color family (at least for your top) is helpful.

Visit onsite if at all possible
Before you accept an offer from a training program it is wise to visit the program. Meet the people. Sit in on classes if you can. Know what you're getting into.

That said, WHERE the program is located really doesn't matter - unless you're relocating a family. You will be in graduate school. You will be incredibly busy. Your graduate school life will likely be the same whether it's in the heart of New York City, in the middle of the desert in Arizona, in Ohio, or in Michigan. Graduate school is incredibly demanding and you won't see much of where you live while attending, so don't pre-judge programs based on where they are located.

Part 4

Interviews: Graduate Training Programs

4-1 Andrei Malaev-Babel
Associate Professor of Theatre
Head of Acting
FSU/Asolo Conservatory for Actor Training

How many students do you accept each year?
Our program is highly selective - we take 12 students each year. Among other things, we are known for our collaboration with the Asolo Repertory Theatre (also known as Asolo Rep) - one of the largest theatres in the South, and one of the few remaining repertory companies in the country. In the third year of training, our students become company members of Asolo Rep. In their first year, they understudy for the Asolo stage. Between these two years, our students earn enough points to join A.E.A. – Actors Equity. We have to consider many different factors when we recruit students for the program. Among them, the needs of the Asolo Rep.

How many do you see in auditions?
We see about 100 people for every student that we accept.

What are your audition requirements?
We follow the URTA requirements – the majority of our students come from the URTA auditions and interviews. These auditions are conducted in late January/early February in Chicago, New York, San Francisco. Many students come to these cities during our recruitment tour in order to audition for us privately. Some students may only be auditioning for select schools, and not attending URTA's (unified auditions and interviews); others would do both URTAs and private auditions. A large number of students only audition at URTAs, relying on callbacks to meet with their schools of choice.

It's common for prospective students to call us a few months in advance to schedule a private audition in one of the three cities. Other students sign up once they are at an URTA hotel. We try to see as many "walk-ins" as we can, although it is an excellent idea to schedule an audition with us in advance – to guarantee being seen.

At URTAs we see the hundreds of prospective students do monologues, and then we call back those individuals who inspire our interest. When we call them back, we ask them to repeat their URTA audition pieces, and often ask to see other pieces they have. This is our chance to work with the students on their pieces, but also to conduct interviews. We only have 15 minutes to accomplish this agenda, and we have to make our decisions based on this rather limited amount of time – about two minutes at URTAs and 15 minutes of callbacks. Which is obviously very difficult. We would rather spend more time with these people, but the intense URTA schedule precludes us from doing so. It definitely helps when students come to us for private auditions, which gives us another 15-20 minutes to work with them, and get to know them. Often, after a callback, we would invite a student to return for a private session. In addition to URTAs, where we recruit 99.9% of our students, we also hold local auditions on our campus in Sarasota. These auditions are attended by Florida residents. Although, we encourage all of our prospective students to come to campus at some point, to see our shows, see the Asolo Rep shows, sit in on classes and chat. It's a great way to get to know us better, although not all of our prospective students can afford to travel to Florida.

When an auditionee walks into the room what are you looking for? When the ideal candidate walks in, what do you see?
I am not one of these people who is going to say that it's all decided as the person walks in, in the first three seconds. There are some people teaching auditioning who say "the moment you walk through the door it's all decided. The first impression, or the first glance decides it all". Our decisions are not based on first glance – they are not even based on the audition pieces. The pieces selected by our prospective students may have nothing to do with a given actor's individual creativity. They may have hired a coach, or they may have coached themselves, in a way that their pieces may not tell us much about them.

We are looking for spontaneous creativity; we try to understand who these young actors *truly* are. Quite often, the "ready product" they've pasted together for an audition is what they rest all their hopes on. We are not necessarily interested in that "wrapped up product" they unwrap in front of us. When they go to the next school, it's going to be exactly the same. My job, as a teacher of acting, is to strip them of everything that they have been coached to do (or that they have coached themselves to do). Everything they've pre-decided must be washed away. My job is to find out their unique and inimitable, fresh, spontaneous, "subconscious" take on the material. I have the technique to do it - to get to that individuality, to get to the core of what they are about. When I manage to do so, I can be pleasantly surprised, or very unpleasantly surprised. I might find out that there is a lot more to this person than what they've been coached to do, or what they have pre-decided this character or monologue is about. Or I can find out in fact that there is much less to that person.

As I said, my job is to find out: what is their intuitive take on the world of the piece? What is their fresh inimitable take on the character: spontaneous and individual, not their intellectual preconception of what the character is. You would be surprised what kind of unexpected things can happen where suddenly an old concept goes out the window, and an intuitive character appears. In most cases, it is much truer to the author, to the text, to the circumstances. In certain cases it is a vivid, fresh, unique, and individual take on the character that is true to the author, but is also based in who this person is as an artist.

As I said, I use special techniques in order to achieve this effect. These are the same techniques I use in training. This gives me a chance to see how a prospective student responds to these techniques. After all, these techniques work best with the actors of certain creative types. For an "experiencing" actor, for an emotional actor, for a spontaneous actor, they are wonderful. For an actor-imitator they are not exactly their cup of tea. As a result, I immediately see two things. I see who this person is in terms of their creative individuality, or at least I begin to see it. (Obviously you cannot see everything in such a short period of time.) And at the same time I see whether they will do well with the kind of techniques I employ in the first year of training.

Following the audition part, we begin to talk with the actors. We ask where they are from, what they like to read, what music they like to listen to, what their hobbies and background are, and whether their parents support their choice to be an actor. (It's not for nothing that you have a section in your book that addresses specifically parents.) It's very important that the parents support this choice, because it's not an easy choice and these young actors will need a lot of support. During these conversations, obviously we try to figure out what they like or dislike in arts, what kind of theater they actually *want to do*. So we do our best in this very limited period of time to find out who this actor is as a person. We learn about their particular tastes and point of view on training. We ask them what they expect from training, and where they see themselves upon graduation from our conservatory. At the same time, we realize that some of these young actors' preconceived ideas about training will quickly change the moment they get the first taste of these very rigorous three years of training. One of the things we have to figure out is whether this person is truly dedicated to the profession. After all, we run a boot camp for actors. Our students' day starts at 9 AM, and they often finish (officially) at 5 PM. Then they go home to do their homework, or go to a rehearsal, or a performance. It's an incredibly rigorous program, so for us to be able to figure out if this person is ready, and serious enough about training, is very important. Are they ready to dedicate three years of their life to nothing but training to be an actor? If we don't learn this during an interview, we might make a mistake of accepting someone who in fact is talented, but is simply not prepared for this kind of an investment of time and effort.

It's very important for us to know what they are going to do (or at least what they think they are going to do) when they graduate because we don't necessarily teach our actors how to become teachers. We are about *practice* - mostly about practice and a way of working. When it comes to teaching opportunities for our students, we don't have many of those. Our strength is giving our students plenty of exposure to working professionals (directors and other actors), and giving them an invaluable experience with professional directors – including directors of highest caliber, like Frank Galati for example. We give our students a chance to become a part of a repertory company in their third year. But we are not putting them in a classroom where they get to teach even in year one - before they have found out what teaching is about or what actor training is about. For somebody who wants to come to graduate school primarily because they want to teach, our program may not be the best place. The best place for them may be a program that is located on a university campus where they're going to get a lot of teaching experience. (We are five hours away from the FSU main campus in Tallahassee, from all our undergraduate theatre programs.) I would however argue that upon completing our training, students might be better equipped to teach just because of how thorough and precise our methods are. This is why many of our students do become fine teachers. At the same time, the majority of them continue to act.

Is there anything that you would like to add to what makes an ideal candidate for your program?
First of all it's an actor who is not interested in faking. Or, better yet – not even very good at faking, but good at developing the role, at experiencing or embodying it - best at becoming the character. Not someone who has some kind of a mental image that they copy, and we end up seeing some mental idea they want to convey by piecing together certain elements of their performance. No, we prefer to work with actors who want to really conceive the part, give birth to the part and become the part - so somebody who, according to Stanislavski's terminology, belongs to the school of "experiencing." Our training is all about that, especially in the first year, and if somebody belongs more to a different school they're just going to have a difficult time with us. They would be much happier and would probably achieve greater results, if they got to work in the vein of their particular talent, their particular gift for imitation, and their particular bent toward what Stanislavsky called the "representational" school of acting. So that is one thing.

The second thing is that we are looking for a certain record of dedication to this profession. Does it mean that we do not accept students who are coming right out of undergraduate school? No, we do accept those actors as well. When we see somebody who recently came out of undergraduate school, but has done lots of theater while in college, or during this year or two after graduation - then it's easier for us to determine: yes, this is a person who is dedicated to making acting their profession. Then this is our type of material.

We are also looking for students who are incredibly open. Those actors who are set in their ways are going to be deeply disappointed - if they get into our program. Because they are going to come here, and they're going to be asked to do everything completely differently than they've been doing it before. The thing is - every teacher is going to ultimately be asking for you to begin from scratch. And that doesn't mean that we're going to "break you and remake you." We are not into breaking and then remaking anybody. But if you are very used to suppressing your creative impulses, if you are very used to constantly acting something *on top of your organic impulses* – then this training is going to be difficult for you at first. Someone who is really open to new ideas and experiences, and ready to just let go of habits and begin to simply listen to what's happening in you *for real* – such a person will do much better than somebody who is not willing to let go of their preconceived ideas.

Then there are other things that just make everybody succeed better in the business. We're connected with the theatre company, which means that our students need to learn how to navigate their own way here. They need to learn to never burn any bridges, to be collegial, to be diplomatic. These things are also worth mentioning, because if somebody is kind of a rebel but does not have the kind of talent that makes one *tolerate* a rebel, it is going to be very difficult for them.

What do you want them to wear to auditions?
I want them to wear something that would inform them, at least on some level, of their characters. Not the way a real costume would. Nevertheless, their attire should give some food to the characters that they've brought to this audition with them. Of course, they do not need to go one hundred percent and show up with a costume. For one thing, they're not going to be doing one character, but two, three, sometimes four different characters, as we ask them: "what else have you got?" This means they need to find one particular "costume" that's going to work for them all. But maybe if they simply think about the kind of characters they are doing... So if I'm a lady wearing heels to an audition, then I should wear the kind of heels I could easily take off and suddenly be barefoot for my next character. If I'm wearing a jacket I could quickly take it off and maybe roll up my sleeves and that would inform me more of my next character. Or, perhaps, for my next character I could pick up the jacket and put it on. So again I'm not going outside of my regular wardrobe, but the choices I have made about my wardrobe give me flexibility. Then this "costume" begins to support who I am going to be as this character or that character. And this would be very interesting and refreshing for an auditor.

I'm not all that interested in seeing a costume that would make a person look sexy or "dashing." I don't want to see a costume that says, "Look at me! Look at what kind of actor I am!" I don't want to see what kind of actor you are - I want to see what kind of characters you are playing. I want to see life on stage. I want to forget about *you* and remember that you're Uncle Vanya or you're Desdemona. I do not want see you wear a costume that constricts your breath or the high heels that make it impossible for you to move.

So how do you do it so that you don't look freakish and don't turn off the auditors? You want to come in ultimately as your authentic self, dressed for a festive occasion. You want to show your respect for the auditors by carefully choosing your attire. As I said, I'm not looking for somebody to dazzle or seduce me with their appearance and looks the moment they walk in. I am actually looking for somebody just simply not to turn me off in any way. The idea is not to make a huge statement "look at me!" But to have an outfit that subtly supports the character when they're doing their monologues - something that is adaptable, transformable, and is completely within the realm of every day life and doesn't reek of theatrical costume. Nevertheless with a slight shift, by losing or gaining some detail of costume, it can easily transform to support the type of pieces that you are doing.

Are there any pieces, monologues, or types of pieces you simply never want to see again?
I don't want to see anything that is just in bad taste – something that is meant to shock me for the sake of

shocking me. I don't want to see an actor curse 40 times throughout the monologue – just for the sake of cursing. I don't want to see anything that is simply not artistically justified. I don't care for this "look at me" kind of thing: "look I can swear in front of these people and not blink an eye"; "I could expose myself"; "I can tackle risqué, scandalous material - I am so progressive and brave!"... And all of that is about "look at me - the actor!"

Also I want them to have cared to read the play. If they don't, they aren't even looking at this monologue as a character, or as a part of the entirety of the play. Sometimes they're just thinking "what a flashy piece! It would be great to say these lines!... What I am saying in these lines, I have no idea. But, boy, these lines are great to say in front of people! And I could be sexy, and I could be tough and I could be..." And now they are merely exploiting these lines for the sake of demonstrating that they can act a certain way. These types of pieces I definitely don't want to see. I don't want to see the pieces where the actor can't even tell who the author is - because it's from a monologue book. They can't even tell me the title of the play. Perhaps there is no play, and, therefore, no true character.

When people come to audition for you, how many pieces do you want them to have prepared?
As many as humanly possible, because we can easily be asking them to do four, even five - especially if we are calling them back. So imagine that you only have two or three... You should have five or six at the least. You should really constantly work on it. But I would suggest, to continue with what I was saying, you shouldn't be

looking at them as pieces, you should be looking at them as characters. And if you're really working on these characters, the pieces will take care of themselves. And if you're working on pieces, characters will never take care of themselves, because characters are parts of a larger whole.

It is probably also important for me to give a disclaimer by mentioning that, unlike many auditors, I am not interested in actors doing their monologues by addressing ghosts, or imaginary partners, or curtains, or windows, or exit signs. I'm interested in them engaging with me.

That is unusual!

It's good for them to know. I am auditioning them for a live stage. I need to know how well they can commune with a partner. Because in our situation they will never be talking to exit signs, they'll never be talking to ghosts, they'll never be talking to curtains, or to lamps in the hotel rooms. They'll be talking to real beings. And their ability to really see that person, to take something from that person, and to give back - it's something I am definitely looking for. So, if I actually told them "no eye contact, I don't exist, choose any point in the space, and do it to that imaginary point," then I'm not seeing the very thing I actually desperately need to see. Some of the greatest actors have said, "I'm only as good as my partner." If I'm not checking that partnership reflex, then I am wasting this precious time. Once again, without the live partner, I am destined to see a piece that has been entirely preconceived. Yes, you can make yourself believe that this curtain is your fiancé - for about a second – and then you will see that it's really a curtain. At that point, you have nothing left but to pretend that you are still seeing a live person in this curtain. Working with an imaginary partner is a kind of level of difficulty that is naïve to expect from somebody who is coming to train for this profession. It's much easier to work with somebody who is alive. [So I have them do their pieces with me as their scene partner.] What does it mean for me? It means that I cannot constantly make notes while they are doing their piece, because if I make notes, I will disengage. Although, the fact that I may disengage for a moment, here and there, should not be a problem for the actor. Do we always look at each other when we converse? No. We often look to the side, or look down, or around… Constant eye contact is not something that's required, or even natural. But a live person that I could speak to is a much easier object to commune with than a lamp, or a window, or a bookcase. This is always the truth for a person who possesses an actor's instinct. And, of course, we are looking for such people. This is yet another thing that distinguishes our way of auditioning, because most of our prospective students are initially surprised by the idea that I want them to speak to me.

So to clarify for the reader: You will watch them do their monologues talking to their Imaginary Other when you see them in the general call. And *then* when they come in to work with you, you will be asking them to do the monologues with you as the scene partner. So it would behoove them to practice doing their monologues to actual human beings, correct?

True.

You cannot imagine what happens! For example, one of the most popular monologues for ingénues is that of the jailer's daughter from *Two Noble Kinsmen* by Shakespeare and Fletcher. Once I had a young actress who came to audition with that monologue. She decided the jailer's daughter is a princess, an aristocratic lady, an extremely refined person. This is how she performed it. She probably did so because one of her prisoners is a nobleman, whom she falls in love with. As she is speaking of his niceties, she assumes the "noble tone." But no simpleton has ever turned into a princess just because she saw a prince. This interpretation was probably due to the fact that the actress never really read the play, or considered the character. She just worked with "the piece." *She* may not have read the play, but *her intuition* did! This is what happened. Having heard the monologue, I said, "Okay, now toss all these lines out of your head, go to the place of emptiness for two or three seconds, and then – green-light the first thing that comes to you. Maybe it's going to be a movement, or a gesture, or the first impression you get from me - because now I am your acting partner. Or, perhaps, in your first moment you will hear a sound – then green light an impression from that sound... Anything will do, as long as this is your first spontaneous impression or sensation. Begin to speak out of this first mood, or impression. No matter where it comes from." The actress did just that – she "emptied," and then followed her first urge, sensation, or impression. Suddenly, she turned into a simple, rough, uneducated wench... she became the jailer's daughter! And the entire monologue began to make sense. When she was done I asked her, "Do you realize you played a completely different character?" She said, "Yes, I guess so!" Then I asked, "Do you realize how much truer this is to the circumstances and to the story? You may be encountering a gentleman, a prince, but you yourself are not of that class. This is the gist, and the humor of the situation!" The actress thought about it and got very excited. But then she went to her next audition and what do you think she did? She did her "gentle woman" – precisely what she prepared before she made this intuitive discovery. I guess, in addition to the intuition, one also has to have a sharp mind that could prompt one that intuition is never wrong.

So yes, you want to prepare for this type of an audition in the way that you prepare for live theatre - with a scene partner who gives you something to work with.

Is there anything else that you would like to add?

Just once more to clarify what kind of an acting training program we are. Above all, we are looking for creative individuals - for the actors who thrive on spontaneous, intuitive creativity. And who have a good head on their shoulders.

4-2 Carla Noack
University of Missouri-Kansas City
Assistant Professor of Acting

Carla Noack: I think the advice for auditioning is, basically, the same across BFA, MFA, URTAs, UPTAs, auditioning for theatre companies - and I think basically it just comes down to *breath*. That's probably the biggest piece of information one can give, the most consistent message you can give. I'm sure you have questions for me but that is something that I would definitely begin with.

What are you looking for when an auditionee walks into the room?
Overall, the thing that I'm looking for the most is a sense of humor. And when I say that it encompasses a lot of

things for me. I assess whether someone knows how to take the work seriously and themselves lightly. How they introduce themselves and put themselves forward is ideally as a wonderful person to spend time with in the room. I want somebody who is humble to the work. And then also somebody who can demonstrate the depth of imagination that shows me that they can dive right in and can release themselves to the work – that's how I put it. And that's a really hard thing to assess, but it is amazing how much you can pick up on just through the little cues that somebody, most of the time unknowingly, gives off that tell us YES - this person has a sense of self, has a confidence and a self-awareness and a sense of their own individual and unique presence, along with an ego-less curiosity.

And so it's like with everything we do, there are so many contradictions to it. To be self-less in the work and also full of self. It's crazy, all the things that we're assessing in those first 90 seconds. But really it takes about 15 seconds to know many, many of these things. So if somebody really just first off *takes time*. Along with a sense of humor, I think part of what I am looking for is that they enjoy listening and they enjoy being listened to. That's become pretty huge for me - that somebody takes the time to listen in the moment. And of course their 90 seconds is not just them coming out on stage and (long pause)... *just listening*. (Laughs) Of course that would be psychotic. But I really like to see somebody who has the presence to just say hello, to greet us, to let us know in that small moment of introduction who they are. Some of my favorite auditions started by people tripping as they walk up on stage, and relaxing themselves, and laughing at themselves. If it's genuine.

In your audition process what do you ask them to prepare?
We go through URTAs, so we match their requirements each year. Generally it's two contrasting monologues and also a song if they're a singer.

When we ask for two contrasting pieces basically it's because we're looking for someone who's able to make a transformational shift somewhere in their audition. So if they wanted to do just one piece that demonstrates their ability to surprise us, to take us to a place that we weren't expecting, that demonstrates their flexibility, then occasionally one piece can do that. But generally it's two contrasting pieces, and we'll usually ask for at least one of those pieces to be classical.

Does "classical" mean Shakespeare to you?
Generally it does, yes. But it's always exciting to see some of the work of Shakespeare's contemporaries in there as well. Generally for me and for most of us at UMKC right now it means Shakespeare, however.

Do you want it to be verse?
That's a good question. Coming into a graduate program, I think verse would demonstrate their skill more completely.

Are there any monologues or types of monologues that you simply never want to hear again?

There were a few years when the *Fat Pig* monologues were everywhere. And I just did not want to see another one of those. But I saw it last year done by a wonderful woman and she did surprise me. As Michael Shurtleff says in his book, the story monologues, those that are basically removing you from the actual action of the monologue, aren't great. I would say unless there's some really active reason you need to tell that story I encourage my students to steer away from those. I think the strongest monologues are the ones that immediately stamp character and immediately let you know what the problem is. Whether it's comedy or tragedy, ideally you're trying to figure out a problem and there's a need *right now* that you have to deal with, so those are the monologues that tend to work the best.

Fat Pig is the only specific one that I would say I don't ever need to see again. I've seen many, many performances, for instance, of the Sonia monologues from *Uncle Vanya*. There are a couple of them that are just so beautiful, and I think last year I saw two of them that were just riveting, just because of the unique perspective that these actors and their imagination brought to the pieces. And that can work for me in a classical sense as well, to see a Chekhov - I would allow that in the classical category.

Do you have any pet peeves at auditions?

I think I have lots of them (smiles). Just *not listening* - somebody that "shows, shows, shows, shows" and just is not allowing anything to go *in*. Everything is coming *out*, nothing is going *in*. What Patsy Rosenberg would call "the Third Circle energy" - everything just coming out!

And then I'd say it is just amazing how inappropriately some actors dress for their auditions. This is not about fashion. I want to know that somebody's body is a means of expression for them. I look first for people to speak from their body, more than from their head. I often tell my students to "live in their knees" so that when they go into their audition they are alive and present to the moment. I'm more interested in that [the body as a means of expression] than I am in their body as just something to look at. There are a lot of gymmed-up people who come into the auditions and they are just super excited to show their abs and their pecs and whatever other muscles they can show off, and there's nothing underneath it. I think that they oftentimes dress as a model would - or as somebody would just trying to show off that well-worked, well-gymmed physique - but the clothing doesn't allow them to really *move*. If they moved in the way that they are supposed to in the monologue, we would see the world! (Laughs) That is really what is most shocking to me. I saw, for example, a woman do Paulina from *A Winter's Tale* and she was up there in the tightest shortest skirt and a tank top and she looked fabulous in a certain way but I knew there was not going to be any "teeth" to the performance, because she's cut off possibilities.

Beautifully put! Thank you!

How many students do you accept into your class each year?
We accept eight.

How many do you audition each year?
Roughly about 800 at URTAs, and then we also have people who come to campus to audition. So it's a good number.

What is the ideal audition outfit? You sort of answered this, but I'll ask the question anyway.
An outfit that allows me to see the person - who they are, what their shape is... But that allows for possibilities, that allows for potential. An outfit that tells me this is a person who can work on the floor, can work elevated, and can go from one thing to another quickly. So I think a perfect outfit would demonstrate that this is somebody who's in the room to work, but there are possibilities for elegance within that. I'm a rolled up shirtsleeves kind of person, but I also know that I've got to bring my elegant self to the work a lot of the time, and there are ways to do that.

Is there anything you want to add?
I'm really interested in a *sense of humor* and a body that's there to *express*, which of course means it needs to be flexible and fit and all of those things for the purpose of expressing.

And I'd say along with that I am interested in people who have a *long-term view of their career as an actor*. So after they've done their pieces, in the callback situation, I'm interested in somebody who's first question is not "are my head shots okay?" and "when do we get to meet agents?" and those kinds of things. I'm interested in the person whose questions are about growing artistically as a creative individual. That really is something you can get a sense of really quickly, and I don't think actors realize that. So part of it really comes down to being savvy about how you communicate. It's about maturity – it's something you grow into as an actor.

I had a student who auditioned for the MFA program and she said, "I want to train now because I believe that I am meant to play the roles of women in their 40s and 50s." Here's this 23-year-old saying this. She had such a long view of the road and she was curious about the process, and the traditions, and the *how*. The flipside of that is so uninteresting to me.

One of the most brilliant pieces of advice I've ever heard is that when you are auditioning you should imagine you are inviting the people in the room, your guests, into your home. Any exercise that gets them to really LOOK at who's behind the table and to really invite them in is great. Just the action of *inviting* is going to call out the technical things like eye contact and breath and those kinds of things as part of a spirit of invitation. I just love that because it puts the auditionee in control. And the auditionee *is* in control!

4-3 Patricia Skarbinski
Northern Illinois University
Head of MFA Acting

What are you looking for as someone begins their audition?
I'm looking for empathy, and intelligence, and curiosity. I'm looking for somebody who's really a student of life and is curious about the human condition. That is evidenced by a lot of things - it's usually evidenced by the way they stand, and the way they speak - the way they hold space. And it's evidenced by the choice of material - I think that's very important. And honestly I make decisions about who to interview based on how they introduce themselves and their pieces. I think I can tell a lot about people by their relationship to their own name. Already from their introduction - how they speak their name and the titles of their chosen material - I know a lot about how they feel about the world and themselves.

Tell me more about that.

Psychologists say the relationship we have with ourselves is the template for the relationships that we have with other people. We cannot have deeper relationships with others than the one we have with ourselves. So the way they say, "hi my name is" tells me a lot: Are they confident? What is their relationship with space? How much energy and presence do they have? How are they taking in others? It gives me an idea of their general worldview. I know it's very quick, but actually I think our brains process information very quickly, and we make assessments extremely quickly, whether we want to admit that or not.

You kind of answered this to some degree, but can you describe what you are looking for in an actor to train?

I'm looking for talent, which means there is a predisposition toward emotional intelligence, the desire to enter into other psychologies outside of our own and a deep, deep imagination. And for someone who has a love for literature and art. I'm looking for people that want to be students, because not everyone wants to learn. So if you want to enter an MFA program you have to really want to be a learner. I'm also looking for people that are going to be good citizens because we are in a small town, we are a three-year MFA program, we recruit once every three years, we largely pay for your education, so we want you to be a good citizen of our school and our community. So that's really important. And then are you hungry? Are you hungry and do you have the potential and the work ethic to be a great actor-artist? I mean, not everybody has that. Of course I am looking for desire and drive, but a lot of what I'm talking about has to do with your capacity for empathy, your intelligence, your ability to communicate using behavior *and* language, and your ability to connect with other people - because that's what we do as actors. And I want to know... are you interested in telling the human story... Do you have originality of thought, creativity? ... So I'm really looking for all of those things.

What are your general audition requirements?
We follow whatever URTA is doing. Right now that includes an introduction and their two pieces.

If people audition at our school, I will not only see their audition, but I will also interview them and usually work with them on their pieces. That helps me determine whether they're a good fit for our program or not.

At URTAs if you call someone back you would also interview them and work their pieces?
We do not usually work their pieces at the URTA auditions, we usually just interview them. I always tell people if you're serious about three years of your life, you have to come and visit us on campus. When they come visit, I will interview them again and I will work with them usually for about an hour. They will also get a chance to sit in on classes, meet other faculty, and talk to current grad students. We try to have as much transparency as possible so that they really know the nature of the program they're getting into bed with (metaphorically). By the end of their visit, which is usually about a two day visit, we will know whether they are a good fit for our program or not. It's important that when a student

chooses a teacher or a program, and a teacher chooses a student, that there is an inherent trust between them. Without that, no learning or transmission of knowledge can take place. There needs to be "animation" between the two people and curiosity about each other's humanity and creative potential. If there's "dead space" between the two of you, you know "this is not my teacher, and I am not their student." And if that is the case, they would really be better served going to a different program and studying with a different teacher.

Are there any monologues or types of monologues that you simply never want to hear again?
No, really there aren't. The choice of monologue tells me what about the human condition are you interested in. And to what level, to what depth, are you willing to investigate? No. As long as you are connected and you are absolutely 100% passionate, this is 100% what you want to say and stand behind, I'm willing to go with you. Most of my issues are with people who are kind of halfhearted about their choices or do not live truthfully under the given circumstances of each piece.

Are you expecting a classical piece in an audition?
It's kind of standard practice. I just want to hear something where there's more complexity of thought, where there's more nuance. I'm a bit more open about what classical means. What I'm looking for is: can a person inhabit epic space, poetic space? As opposed to something a little bit more colloquial or daily.

So you would like to hear heightened text?
Yes. Which comes from an ability to inhabit heightened space in one's life. That means connecting to things that are bigger than our commerce-driven existence of today. Its about tapping into that ability and desire to speak to the gods, let's say...or address ancestors...or awaken the spirits from the dead; or the need to talk of Death, or war, Famine and injustice, or love, or ecstasy, or purity of heart... It's when our daily language fails us, and we need to bump up into a language and form that can encompass more - that can express more. It can be through verse like in Shakespeare, or through more open, poetic forms like we sometimes find in many contemporary translations of ancient Greek plays. Or perhaps simply through the more elaborate use of imagery and metaphor. Either way, it's about embodying poetic space.

What is the ideal monologue length?
One minute. Maybe a minute and 15 seconds if you need it. More than a minute and a half I don't need to see. I can tell you within 30 seconds if I'm interested in the person and in watching. Or not.

What is the ideal audition outfit? Or what is it not?
I think trendy clothes are very bad for auditioning - they obscure the person. I would really l18e somebody who understands their body and how best to show it off. Meaning the outside should represent the inside (who you actually are, your essence.) So don't wear trendy clothes simply because they're popular. I would very happily see a woman in a long skirt, a belt, and a nice blouse if that's really helping her express who she

actually is. It's great if people can see an image consultant and understand their colors and understand their body type and what does and does not work best for them. Oh! I will say - I hate baby doll dresses. Please, women, never wear them because they visually undermine your power, maturity, and complexity.

Also, can you please wear shoes in which you can be grounded? I just don't want clothing that presents a *mask*. I do appreciate people getting dressed up. I think casual too soon is not a good message. Why don't we earn casual with each other? Let's be formal first and let's earn casual. So it's got to be revealing of who you are, but I also want to feel like you made an effort in what you presented to us.

Can you clarify formal? What does formal mean?
Formal means to me that you have put care and thought into what you wore. It is a choice and the choice is based on the fact that I want to best reveal who I am. I am not hiding behind my clothing. I am not maximizing, I am not trying to make myself more into something that I'm not, or less than what I am. But at the same time I dressed with care. I want to feel like people put an effort into their presentation.

Beautifully put.

Is there anything you want to add for people auditioning for your program? Or about auditioning, in general?
Yes. Figure out what you want in life because it's short. And be hungry and passionate. Figure out what you want

to talk about as an artist. And then choose pieces that address that. And reveal your struggles, reveal your weaknesses, reveal your inconsistencies. You know, it's the polished mask that most makes us feel inhuman. Because we feel like "God I could never live up to that, I don't have a polished mask. I'm full of weaknesses and insecurities and yet great passion." So yes, I need complexity, and I need nuance, and I need somebody who really wants to be doing this.

4-4 Philip Thompson
University of California, Irvine

How many people do you recruit into each class?
Eight.

And you are an URTA school?
Yes.

When the ideal candidate for your program walks into the room what do you see?
Well we hope that I'm actually aware that they're the ideal candidates! I'm really careful about trying not to come up with any canned answers for myself - as a way of preventing skipping to some automatic heuristic that says they have to have "these qualities." This allows me to be surprised by somebody who compels me to be interested in him or her for reasons that I haven't yet thought through.

I'll also say now that the prospect of giving advice about auditioning leaves me with a little bit of anxiety because I don't want to come up with automatic "ready for every purpose" answers because every situation and every individual is a little bit different.

So, enough preamble. Here's what I see:

I see somebody who sees and engages with their imaginary scene partner. That's the bottom line. If they don't show me that they have the ability to be changed by that imaginary person, then I know that they don't have the imagination or the mental freedom to learn how, finally, to be an actor.

I do some checking about their physical skills and strengths, their quickness of mind, their ability to take direction - even sometimes kind of stupid direction - so that I can see whether or not they're actually listening. I am trying to imagine them as a working actor. And also as somebody who might act alongside the students that I already have. That does mean that I am inviting in my biases to say, "Well this 'blonde bombshell' looks like the sort of person who could have her own TV series" for example. So I am swayed by looks and type to a certain degree. But that is something that I am fighting against as well.

Could you talk about what you mean when you say type?
Yes. One learns about type by seeing the sorts of people that are in the stories we watch. They do fall into categories: based on temperament, based on readiness to use certain tactics, whether they tend toward overpowering people or being victimized by people. And also there are certain archetypes at work as well. It's not a deal-breaker, but if somebody who is big and goofy has the sensibility towards the leading man's simplicity with moment-to-moment playing, and he doesn't have a sensibility (this big goofy imaginary actor) toward also being goofy, then there is a mismatch between his look and his sensibilities or temperament. We all know that somebody like Paul Giamatti both looks his type and can play his type, but he also has a tremendous capacity towards all sorts of other things.

So I guess in the end, my ideal candidate is dead center of their type with the potential to do something surprising that's outside their type.

Do you expect to hear Shakespeare?
I *like* to hear Shakespeare. It's certainly the case that the URTA structure - and most people follow that structure because we are looking at most people through the URTA auditions - prescribes what is expected in the audition. There's a request for contrasting pieces and that one of them should be in verse, which is a very sneaky way of asking for something. I don't think most people really care or can even necessarily tell, whether it's actually in prose or verse. But what they want is language that is elevated and complex. In order to see the different ways the actor engages with language I want to see them tackle some complex and archaic language and naturalize it, and I also want to see them deal with some contemporary language. So for the complex and rhetorically structured language, why not choose Shakespeare because he's awesome! That's my point of view. Now if somebody brings in a little bit of Beaumont and Fletcher or a Restoration play that can work, too. One should be aware that it does not always work to choose the Greeks because translations can shortchange the complexity of language. There might be complexity of argument and there might be grand feeling, but the thing that I want in classical work and Shakespeare is not its operatic qualities, but the intellectual rigor and the combination of passion and intelligence. And gosh, you just can find it right there in Shakespeare, so why not do that?

I betray my prejudices.

What is the ideal audition outfit?
An audition outfit is a 'costume.' The part you're playing is the part of the really well put together, thoughtful actor who likes to look nice. You are not trying to play the part of a public accountant on casual Friday. You're trying to look sharp, but like you happened to wake up like this. So it's really essential that people do put a lot of thought into their 'costume,' but not in order to fit some ideal that's out there for their imaginary auditor, but to say "look, if I was a successful and super-cool actor, and I liked to look nice when I went out and did my job, this is what I'd wear." I don't want to see either board shorts on the one extreme, or a starched blue button-down shirt that's never been worn before on the other extreme. Because those are mismatches of informality and formality at either end of the scale. And finally it's not the formality of the situation that is the most interesting to me; it's the *coolness* of the situation that's most interesting to me, the *tastefulness* of the situation.
(Smiles)

You will find that all of my answers are evasive like this because every interesting answer is ambiguous and complicated.
(Smiles)

Do you have any pet peeves?
My pet peeve is having pet peeves. Sometimes people have opinions that solidify into "rules." I do have objections to some things that I see, and obviously the main objection I have is just not doing the "acting" part

right - not really talking to a person, not really responding to a person, or simply declaiming. I can't call that a pet peeve – it's me just not liking the fact that they are not doing their job as actors.

What sorts of things do you object to?
I think sometimes people treat Shakespeare with an excessive formality of language and they do a certain quasi-English accent - and that *does* annoy me.

I do object pretty strongly to people not having memorized the language thoroughly. Especially in Shakespeare. If it's a contemporary piece that they have mis-memorized, I probably won't notice, but maybe I will (usually because what came out of your mouth was a piece of nonsense.) It is obvious when people with not a lot of experience with 400 year old language pick up the material and read it wrong - because they are expecting to see a different set of words. People just saying the words without actually attending to what the words are meant to do peeve me. If they've memorized it wrong and are adding extra words in, then they aren't doing the text and that means they're missing a great opportunity to use a really well built piece of machinery! They're substituting their *#%**# piece of cardboard for the beautifully made marble that they've been offered.

Are there things that you think people auditioning should know?
I think that people have to know what their job is and what the context of the audition really is. On one level they should know what the room is like, what the expectations are, and who's going to be there so they are

232

not freaked out by the newness of it. But also they should know what it's all for: what the slating of the name is for, and what the real relationship is between you and the person on the other side of the table. I think they often misunderstand and see it as sort of "judges panel," which it's not. Or auditionees may see the auditors as a group of teachers - and because they are not giving you feedback, they are not teaching you anything. It's really that you as the auditionee and these other people have come together in a room to see if they can find potential for great acting. And if you know that the people on the other side of the table are there looking to see if you offer the possibility for having a talented student who can learn, then the pressure is off of you. You are just doing your job as an actor, and these other people are also interested in you doing your job. And the job is to respond to imaginary people and imaginary circumstances. And if you can do that then people will be able to see it.

You might think "I've got to do it right" when your doing it "right" has pretty much zero to do with whether or not you get cast or selected. There are so many reasons out there for why people make the choices they do that the only thing that you can really attend to is, "Am I engaging with this acting problem well?" It's up to the auditors to say, "Yeah, we need one of those, and we need one of those..." They are doing selecting and you are doing creating. They are not judging your work. When people get out of the mindset of believing that someone is judging their work, they start to do really good work and they start to have a lot of love left over for the people on the other side of the table.

Because I have heard you talk about this, I would like you to talk about figuring out what you have to offer - what it is that makes you unique. Could you talk about that?
Yes. It lies inside the dangerous idea of "type," which we've mentioned previously. There are some categories that have to do with what you are likely to play. Type sometimes feels like something other people "put on you." I wouldn't recommend that way looking at it. For example, a few years ago I was a feckless kid - a little lovable, bumbling poet, quite ready to cry, and youthful, and cute. And that's the way people read me and that was pretty dead on, But if I think my only job as an actor is to tell you that that is my type, then I start getting into all sorts of games in my head. Type is never something outside of you that you're trying to fulfill, but it might be a convenient way for people to think about your category. They may say "oh yeah, this is the guy who would be cast in this kind of role." People do need shortcuts, and you should be aware of those shortcuts and you should be ready to accentuate or de-accentuate aspects of yourself in order to make that super clear for people. I think that is a valid thing for actors to do. To say "I seem to be the bubbly cute girl, and that's the way people are reading me, and these are the aspects of myself that make that happen."

But you should also be aware of what your unique response to a text is and the things about you that might be interesting to other people. Now this level of introspection about yourself can be uncomfortable, but fortunately actors are already a little more narcissistic than the rest of the population, so this should give you an opportunity to really *enjoy* thinking about what is "you." Yes, people will look at you and they will view you in the traditional roles. And that's the mechanism by which a lot of bias occurs in this world - the reason why African-Americans, for example, in film and stage, are often given a paltry set of characters to play. It's why gender disparities in drama are so terrible - it's because people have an idea of an 'important scientist' and they only think of a man in that role. And so that is a problem of type. If you really know yourself and you can read for something that's out of type according to what "The Man" thinks, then you might be able to be the engine for increasing the variety of stories that get told. So it's not just narcissism, it's really about saying, "I have something to say." And because actors are often in a position of asking if they could perhaps-please-have-the-opportunity-to-get-to-say-somebody-else's-words so much, they often forget that *it's important for them to have something to say*. And that I think is how you find who you really are: by practicing stating your opinions. By putting yourself out there.

I have another thought about this. Sometimes we have things we view as negative about ourselves, things that could be taken as criticisms... such as "you are way too apologetic," for example... that may be true. But it might also be your super power. You might be the person who they go to when they need an apologetic person. You might be super good at that. So your weakness is your strength potentially. Because there are all sorts of characters that get played, not just the people we've idealized as "good people." Everything within you is a potential super power that you can nurture and become the skillful master of. If you deny things about yourself or put them in the category of "stuff you want to change and fix" then you won't have access to them when you might need them.

I have one last thing to say about this. My colleague, Richard Brestoff, says this. Very often the Hollywood Machine will pick up on your type. And that's probably because who you are and what you look like and what you are comfortable with all line up around an already known cluster of personality traits. And they will take that and they will squeeze it out of you, and then when they are done with that they will look at you and say, "Do you have anything else to offer?" And if you don't have anything else, because you've suppressed it or you defined it as not worthy, then you're screwed. Because they are moving on to one of the other 150,000 possibilities and you are done. So if you are an indie songwriter or a mad scientist or a veterinarian in your heart, then keep all those sensibilities alive in you so that you can be good and flexible at making your art. Sometimes people think of themselves in the role of 'actor' and that becomes the only thing that they ever practice: being an actor. When, in fact, actors need to have access to all sorts of stuff because you are going to play all sorts of people. You want to have personal depth. Someday you are going to have to play a truly complex person, and you'd better still have your own complexities or you're going to be just making stuff up and that's always boring.

4-5 Phil Timberlake
The Theatre School at DePaul University
Associate Professor of Voice and Speech

Phil Timberlake auditions and recruits for both the BFA Acting and MFA Acting programs.

It would be wise to read the entirety of the interview in the BFA section, as the majority of that information applies to auditions for both programs.

This material is specifically for MFA candidates.

Audition requirements
The MFAs come in with two pieces: a contemporary monologue and a classical monologue. Then we interview them.

And then we also do the same things with them as the BFA audition - a little bit of voice and movement and scene work, to see them work and also for them to get to know how *we* work. Coming back to school can be a shocking experience. And then we do open scene work as well. So there are slightly different requirements for what MFA candidates bring in. But overall what we are trying to do is get to know people in a classroom kind of experience.

When you say classical, do you mean Shakespeare?
It should be in verse. Most people do Shakespeare. So Shakespeare, Molière, Restoration, etc.

If they do Shakespeare do you prefer verse?
Yes, the classical piece needs to be in verse for our auditions.

Is there anything you want to add?
For the MFA's I would say really ask yourself, "Why am I applying to an MFA program? And why this program? And why now?" Because an MFA program, or even auditioning for an MFA program, can simply be a way of avoiding the hard reality of your future. And maybe it's just simply the sense that you don't know what comes next. Now that doesn't mean that you shouldn't audition, but you should ask yourself those questions. Because those are important, important questions to ask.

4-6 Walton Wilson
Yale School of Drama
Head of Voice and Speech
Chair, Department of Acting

What population do you audition?
We are strictly a graduate school. There is an undergraduate theatre studies program at Yale, but we are completely separate from them.

When an auditionee walks in the room what are you looking for initially from them?
I mean, it's such a subjective thing isn't it? When they enter, my radar just peaks a little bit.

What we do in our auditions is we schedule so many people each hour. Let's say maybe 12 to 14 people. I'm in one room, my partner Ron Van Lieu is in the other room. What we do each hour is we bring the entire group in together. And we talk to them for about five minutes, try to relax them, talk about what this process is, etc. etc. And then we see them individually.

I'm looking for someone who seems to understand that the audition room belongs to the actor. I'm only there because someone's walked into the room, right? So it is very attractive when an actor takes agency in the room. When they come in they are there to do their work. They don't seem eager to please me in one way or another. I think it's nice to be cordial. It's nice for the person to acknowledge me, because I greet everyone who comes into the room. You know, just to have a moment of "here we are in this room together." So someone who appears to be in charge of themselves, and confident in what they're doing - that's a good sign. We see many, many people during the course of our audition season. So after the first day, during which we had a chance to acclimate and say "OK this is where the bar is," it doesn't take very long for me to know if a person may not be right for the program. If they can hold my interest, that's a good sign. If they can just keep holding my interest... And some people do!

It doesn't matter to me what their choice of material is, really. People always ask "what kind of material should I bring in?" and I think the answer is that it should be something that you feel really drawn to, something that reveals *you*. And it's easy to tell when the person who's up there understands who they are through the choice of their material. And you *have* to - in order to take advantage of what we do at Yale - you *have* to know who you are. You have to have some of the big questions already answered. Because it's too difficult trying to figure out who you are and trying to act at the same time. So that when they're showing themselves, or when they get down to work, it feels like "this is who I am." That's what I'm looking for. Is this person revealing themselves, rather than trying to show off that they have some skill? Because showing off "skill" is not particularly interesting in that context. Does that answer that question?

Yes. Yes it does. You actually answered a couple of questions there!

At this point in time what are your audition requirements?
We want two contrasting pieces, five minutes. One piece - something from a modern or contemporary play. One piece - Shakespeare, and we really prefer that it's verse rather than prose. And they should have two more pieces in their pocket. It's a good thing in an audition when someone asks to see another piece. It means we want to see something different, something more. And those additional pieces should also be Shakespeare verse or contemporary.

So to clarify, they should come in with two Shakespeare verse and two contemporary pieces.
Yes. And that's plenty.

Any monologues that you absolutely never want to hear again?
Let me put it this way, there are monologues that I've never seen work in an audition situation. And I would be happy never to see them again. Then again there's always a first time! If someone is really, really, really

drawn to playing Launce and his dog then... OK! But, I find that to be a challenging piece to make work, for example. But I don't want to circumscribe the material that an actor wants to bring in out of fairness to them. And you know, it's just two minutes of my life!

How many students do you accept into your program each year?
Generally 16.

How many do you see, roughly?
1000.

Do you have any pet peeves at auditions?
I've been doing this for a number of years... I think when I was younger at it, when I was starting out at it, I did. But I think in retrospect what happened is that when someone stepped on that "land mine," as it were, that probably prevented me from seeing something there. If I automatically dismissed that person that may have been my loss in some instances. My goal is to absolutely be present with these people so I don't... look... if something is really unwatchable I can always leave my body. (Smiles)

We give guidelines when they come in the room. We show them a tape mark and explain that all that territory is theirs and all this territory is ours. Because it helps us to see them better, with a little distance. And we ask people very explicitly not to directly address us because we can't be their scene partners. We are working while they are working. We are looking up and down, making notes, etc. Sometimes people are in such a state of anxiety that they don't hear that - or they're just not in control of themselves. So they'll advance right up to the table, stare me in the eyes, and proceed to yell at me. And it's like, "I'm leaving my body now," and then when it's over I come back.

You know, when I was younger, I would think poorly of people when they did that. But now I understand - they're so nervous, they're so 'aaaah' that they probably can't take anything in. Which is too bad, but that's the way it is. And you learn. You learn by doing.

What is the ideal audition outfit?
I suppose it's like what people talk about with a good headshot: it should be you on a good day. I think it's good when someone is groomed, when their clothes are clean, they aren't wearing cut offs and showing me all their ink, or if they do have ink they hide it. You know, as they say in the south, "someone who's made an effort." You should be comfortable and clean. Probably wear a shirt with a collar.

I think for women… and this is a huge generalization of course… it's maybe more likely that they'll come in overdressed: a lot of make up, a lot of jewelry, tight fitting clothes. Sometimes doesn't serve them with the material that they're doing, they have a hard time moving or breathing because of the way the clothes are constructed.

I just seem to notice if someone looks uncomfortable in their clothing.

How long is the ideal monologue?

In terms of time? Typically on the last weekend that we hold auditions in New Haven, it coincides with the URTA auditions in New York. So we'll see a lot of URTA auditions that weekend, which means these guys blow into the room, they're talking a mile a minute because they're trying to cram it all into their allotted time... And it's ridiculous! Because I can't see anything! I can't tell anything. You know, I feel very sorry for them - I don't know what I'm watching - people aren't "living through" anything, they're just trying to get it all in under a minute. Whatever that crazy time limit is.

To be honest, if I know I'm not interested in someone, it's too long [the monologue].

If someone's interesting to me, I want to keep watching. It's just a very subjective feeling.

Well, auditing is subjective.

Completely subjective.

Is there anything that has come to you that you would like to add?

I suspect this is probably true of actors in every audition situation, but I think it's a waste of time and energy to try to tailor what you're doing to what you think that person [the auditor] wants to see. "What do they want? What do they like?" Well, you have no idea what I'm thinking. It's like in the theatre - you have no clue what the audience is thinking! They may be thinking about your shoes. You have no control over it.

Also... the person on one side of the table and the person on the other side of the table *actually want the same outcome*. They want the same thing. So rather than thinking "they're just here to judge me or tell me how sucky I am," remember we all want the same thing. For whatever reason, young actors often perceive it as an adversarial relationship. And it's not at all.

Everyone who sits on the auditor side of the table has a problem: they have this role they have to cast, or this class they need to find good actors for. So on a very deep level, people want you to succeed when you walk into the room. I think if you can put that thought into your mind, that you are actually *wanted*, that's a much more practically useful way to come into the room.

Part 5

For
Parents
And
Supportive
Others

5-1 For the parents who are scared

Begin by reading "What will you learn as a theatre major? Ten reasons to study theatre" (in Part 1)

I know it can seem scary for your child to go into the arts. The world we live in does not really champion the arts and it seems like a riskier proposition financially than a career in business.

There are more careers in theatre, film, and television than the general population knows about. Watch the credits at the end of the movie next time. Many of those people have theatre degrees and most of them are very well paid. Do some reading about the business. Don't assume that if your child doesn't make it as an actor, he or she will have no future in this art form. It's a very big art form with many different roles.

As an acting teacher, I cannot tell you how impressed I am with the things our students learn about themselves, human nature, and the world around them as theatre majors. They work at an intense level. It is often stressful. And they learn to WORK HARD.

Will they all become famous? Will they all choose to be professional actors? No. Not everyone ends up working in the career for which they earned their degree. That is true of all majors, by the way. But they take the skills they learn as actors and artists into whatever career they choose and those skills help them excel. Of this I have no doubt.

I am a practical person. And I was hesitant about going into the arts. I started in marketing and I tried for a long time to be a "normal" person. And I was not happy. Finally, after years of trying everything else, I returned to acting and found a way of life that allowed me to be myself (paradoxically, through the experience of being lots of different people.) I spent years in school in other majors and a lot of time trying many different things before I finally just admitted that a career in theatre is what I truly wanted and until I did it I would not be honoring the person I was created to be.

At the time of this writing, my son is in college. He is not a theatre major, but if he were I would be fine with that. His major is another that is often considered an "impractical" undergraduate degree, but I don't worry about that at all. He is pursuing something he is passionate about. He may never make tons of money and may never retire young. So what? If he is doing what he loves, work that feeds him, retirement isn't a big deal. I know this from my own experience. My work brings me joy now. If he finds joy in his work, that is what matters to me.

You may have a view that is very different from mine. If the idea of your child going into the arts terrifies you, encourage them to minor in something. They may even do a double major (though the workload inherent in a theatre degree can make this challenging.) But please honor who they are - and in who you raised them to be - enough to also encourage them to pursue their dreams.

5-2 How you can help your son or daughter in the audition process

The best thing we, as parents, can do is to stay as much out of the way as possible. I know that's hard. But it's important. Just as there are parents who get "too involved" in coaching their kids from the stands in Little League games, there are parents who get overly involved in their kid's audition process.

Offer support and encouragement only – and only if asked. Making corrections and giving advice is tricky. The fact is, you really don't know what the auditors are looking for. As you read interviews you'll find they are not looking for a slick, professional entrance and performance. It's not like a job interview. And truthfully, most parents tend to steer their children toward more of a "performance" than the auditors want to see.

To be completely frank, even though I coach for a living – professionals and students – if my child were auditioning for acting training programs I would not be his coach. If he needed a coach I would encourage *him* to hire someone – and it wouldn't be me.

No one can own another's artistic process. It is highly individual. You might be surprised at what type of help or coaching your child best responds to. If they did hire their own coach, they might hire someone you absolutely would never hire!

Ideally, auditionees need to prepare on their own or with the guidance of a teacher or coach. As you have read throughout this book, auditors can tell a great deal about auditionees based on the material they select and how they prepare it. So ideally THEY select it and THEY prepare it.

5-3 When it comes to dealing with the program...

If you have questions for training program personnel, ask them in the appropriate venue and at the appropriate time. On site at the audition is not the time to ask questions unless time is set aside to answer questions from parents and supportive others.

The auditors should know your child better than they know you. As a parent I completely understand the idea of wanting to smooth the way for your kid, but that is ill advised in this process. There may be places in life where that is ok, but a theatrical training community is not one of them. If your child is accepted into a program, he or she will be training with the faculty without you in the room. Actors considering a training program need to know how it feels to work with the trainers at that program, and the audition is part of that. This is the first step. It's one of the ways your child will learn what it will feel like to be treated as an adult and asked to take ownership of their own creative process.

As I was interviewing auditors, the issue of how parents help and hurt auditionees came up several times. Different programs have different approaches. Some programs do not allow parents to watch classes because they want the prospective student to experience what it is to be in the training space and a part of the atmosphere of the program without the influence of their parents. Some programs ask parents not to even enter the building on audition days.

Several times auditors mentioned that they are very aware of when a child is being berated or drilled by a parent outside the audition room, and they are very aware that this influences the audition negatively.

Two auditors flatly stated that they have simply not accepted some actors because a parent was overly involved. They knew accepting that actor would mean four years of dealing with the actor's parent, and that was a dynamic they wanted to avoid.

Once your son or daughter is accepted into a program, THEN it makes sense to ask questions that have not been answered. Once an actor has been accepted into a program via the audition process and is being actively recruited, information is very easy to get!

Interviews to read
Auditor interviewees Jim Daniels and David Williams specifically shared information parents may want to review. Take a look at their interviews.

5-4 For the kids of parents who are scared

Your parents love you.

They want the best for you.

They are thinking about you and your future.

They want you to be successful, and happy, and to be able to pay your own bills.

Even if they seem to not understand you and your dreams sometimes, please realize *they are on your side!*

Now, go forth and…

Break a leg!!!

Acknowledgements

My own teachers are numerous and surely I would miss someone if I attempted to mention them all. You know who you are and you are magnificent. I offer special recognition to Raedene VandenHeuvel, Frank Hunter, Paul Nicholas, and Rick Kuebler, all of whom are no longer with me in body, but have no doubt been reading over my shoulder as I wrote - and hopefully whispering in my ear. I also offer special thanks to Kathryn Gately, Catherine Fitzmaurice, and Karina Ayn Mirsky, who not only continue to bless me as teachers, but have shaped organizations that carry their work forward, thereby blessing others as well.

To the auditors who graciously agreed to be interviewed for this book: I am forever grateful to you. I deeply appreciate your time, your energy, your openness, and your dedication to the training of artists. You made this process a pleasure.

Thank you to my proofreaders and angels of input: Dee and Wanda Hickman, Kate Thomsen, and Nel Steffens.

Thank you to Sarah West, who did the cover photography, and to models Alex Oparka and Eddie Coleman III.

To my colleagues and friends at Western Michigan University: I am deeply thankful for your kindness, professionalism, support, and friendship.

To my students and clients (past and present): You add such joy to my life. Thank you for your open hearts, open minds, and for your expansive, expressive spirits.

To my many cheerleaders and encouraging friends, including Maile, Michelle, Meghan, Nel (your turn!), Elisa, Laura, Cheryl, Cheri, Marissa, Patricia, Edwin, Bianca, Joan, Tanisha, Chelsea, Eva, Julie, Terri, and Sophie: YOU ROCK!

And thank you to Isaac for your encouragement, support, understanding, and willingness to share me with all my nutty actor friends.

About the Author

Elizabeth Terrel
Western Michigan University
Director of Voice & Movement

Elizabeth Terrel Coaching®, Chicago, Illinois

Elizabeth Terrel is an actor/singer, a private coach, and a professor. She holds an MFA in Acting from Northern Illinois University where she trained with Kathryn Gately. She is an Associate Teacher of Fitzmaurice Voicework®, a yoga instructor (RYT500), and the creator of Terrel Presence Training®.

Ms. Terrel is also a certified personal image consultant who specializes in working with artists, actors, and gender embodiment.

She is a proud member of AEA (Actors Equity Association), SAG-AFTRA (Screen Actors Guild-American Federation of Television and Radio Artists), VASTA (Voice and Speech Trainers Association),

ATHE (Association for Theatre in Higher Education), and ATME (Association of Theatre Movement Educators).

Visit elizabethterrelcoaching.com to read the ETC Blog, access additional material, and find information about other publications.

CPSIA information can be obtained
at www.ICGtesting.com
Printed in the USA
FSOW01n2359020117
29141FS